VGM's

HANDBOOK

of SCIENTIFIC

&

TECHNICAL

CAREERS

VGM's HANDBOOK *of* SCIENTIFIC & TECHNICAL CAREERS

edited by Craig T. Norback

VGM Career Horizons
a division of *NTC Publishing Group*
Lincolnwood, Illinois USA

Library of Congress Cataloging-in-Publication Data

VGM's handbook of scientific and technical careers / edited by Craig T.
Norback.
     p.   cm.
   ISBN 0-8442-8823-3 : $12.95
   1. Engineering—Vocational guidance.   2. Science—Vocational
guidance   3. Technology—Vocational guidance.   I. Norback, Craig
T.   II. VGM Career Horizons (Firm)
TA157.V46   1989
602.3—dc20   89-37395
                                                                CIP

Published by VGM Career Horizons, a division of NTC Publishing Group.
© 1990 by NTC Publishing Group, 4255 West Touhy Avenue,
Lincolnwood (Chicago), Illinois 60646-1975 U.S.A.
Manufactured in the United States of America.

9 0 VP 9 8 7 6 5 4 3 2 1

Contents

Contents

How to Use This Book

VGM's Handbook of Scientific and Technical Careers contains vital information on 50 popular careers in science and technology. Each career has been carefully researched and described in text that is easy to understand. The careers are listed in alphabetical order for easy reference, and each is described in the following fashion:

◇ *The Job.* A general description of what the job is like and what persons in the field are expected to do.

◇ *Places of Employment and Working Conditions.* Where major employers in the field are located and what type of work environment to expect, i.e. office work, outdoor work, urban location, rural location. Typical working hours are also given.

◇ *Qualifications, Education, and Training.* How to qualify for a job in the field, what type of education is necessary, and any special training that may help you get a start in the field.

◇ *Potential and Advancement.* The approximate number of persons employed in the field nationwide, projections on whether the field will grow or shrink in the upcoming years, and typical paths of advancement for workers.

◇ *Income.* The most current salary figures available, for beginners in the field and for experienced workers. Keep in mind that such figures are subject to change, due primarily to supply and demand within the labor force and to inflation. Be sure to check with various employers and associations for the most recent figures while conducting your job search.

◇ *Additional Sources of Information.* Names and addresses of associations and other groups that can supply more information about careers in the field. These organizations can be very helpful, so be sure to contact them if you need additional information.

This handy reference book allows you to compare and contrast various careers in science and technology all within one volume. You can use it to find out about fields that may already interest you, or you can read it cover to cover in order to explore a variety of career paths that you might find appealing.

The appendix in the back of the book helps you with résumés, application forms, cover letters, and interviews. Once you have settled on a particular career path, be sure to use this information to prepare yourself to go after a job.

Aerospace Engineer

The Job   The design, development, testing, and production of commercial and military aircraft, missiles, and spacecraft are the duties of aerospace engineers. Their work is important to commercial aviation, national defense, and the space program.

Aerospace engineers often specialize in one area such as structural design, instrumentation and communications, or production methods. They may also specialize in one type of product such as helicopters, satellites, or rockets.

Most aerospace engineers are employed by aircraft and aircraft parts manufacturers. The National Aeronautics and Space Administration and the Department of Defense employ 20 percent of American aerospace engineers, and a few work for commercial airlines and consulting firms.

Places of Employment and Working Conditions   The aerospace industry is concentrated in Florida, Texas, and on the West Coast.

Qualifications, Education, and Training   The ability to think analytically, a capacity for details, and the ability to work as part of a team are all necessary. Good communication skills are important.

Mathematics and the sciences must be emphasized in high school. A bachelor's degree in engineering is the minimum requirement in this field. In a typical curriculum, the first two years are spent in the study of basic sciences such as physics and chemistry and mathematics, introductory engineering, and some liberal arts courses. The remaining years are usually devoted to specialized engineering courses.

Engineering programs can last from four to six years. Those that require five or six years to complete may award a master's degree or may provide a cooperative plan of study plus practical work experience with a nearby industry.

Because of rapid changes in technology, many aerospace engineers continue their education throughout their careers. A graduate degree is necessary for most teaching and research positions and for many management jobs. Some persons obtain graduate degrees in business administration.

All states require licensing of engineers whose work may affect life, health, or property or who offer their services to the public. Those who are licensed, about one-third of all engineers, are called registered engineers. Requirements for licensing include graduation from an accredited engineering school, four years of experience, and an examination.

Potential and Advancement   There are about 53,000 aerospace engineers. New employment opportunities in this field are not expected in the near future unless the federal government increases its spending on defense and space exploration. Most job openings will occur to replace those who retire or leave the field.

Income   Starting salaries for engineers with the bachelor's degree are significantly higher than starting salaries of college graduates in other fields. According to the College Placement Council, engineering graduates with a bachelor's degree and no experience averaged about $27,900 a year in private industry in 1986; those with a master's degree and no experience, $33,100 a year; and those with a Ph.D., $42,200. Starting offers for those with the bachelor's degree vary by branch.

Additional Sources of Information

American Institute of Aeronautics and Astronautics
370 L'Enfant Promenade SW
Washington, DC 20024

Engineers' Council for Professional Development
345 East 47th Street
New York, NY 10017

National Society of Professional Engineers
1420 King Street
Alexandria, VA 22314

American Society for Engineering Education
11 Dupont Circle
Suite 200
Washington, DC 20036

Society of Women Engineers
United Engineering Center
345 East 47th Street
New York, NY 10017

Agricultural Engineer

The Job Agricultural engineers design and develop a variety of products and services for farmers, ranchers, and the agricultural industry.

Agricultural engineers may design the most effective layout for a farm including placement of barns and irrigation systems; others design specific buildings such as dairy barns. Utility companies employ agricultural engineers to develop electrical power systems for farms and food processing companies. Manufacturers of farm equipment and machinery employ them in design and development as well as in sales.

The federal government employs agricultural engineers in soil and water management projects and as cooperative extension service agents, most of them in the Department of Agriculture.

Places of Employment and Working Conditions Agricultural engineers work mainly in rural areas and their work is often done out-of-doors.

Qualifications, Education, and Training The ability to think analytically, a capacity for details, and the ability to work as part of a team are all necessary. Good communication skills are important.

Mathematics and the sciences must be emphasized in high school.

A bachelor's degree in engineering is the minimum requirement in this field. In a typical curriculum, the first two years are spent in the study of basic sciences such as physics and chemistry and mathematics, introductory engineering, and some liberal arts courses. The remaining years are usually devoted to specialized engineering courses.

Engineering programs can last from four to six years. Those requiring five or six years to complete may award a master's degree or may provide a cooperative plan of study plus practical work experience with a nearby industry.

Because of rapid changes in technology, many agricultural engineers continue their education throughout their careers. A graduate degree is necessary for most teaching and research positions and for many management jobs. Some persons obtain graduate degrees in business administration or in an agricultural field such as soil science or forestry.

All states require licensing of engineers whose work may affect life, health, or property or who offer their services to the public. Those who are licensed, about one-third of all engineers, are called registered engineers. Requirements for licensing include graduation from an accredited engineering school, four years of experience, and an examination.

Potential and Advancement   There are about 15,000 agricultural engineers and the field is expected to show substantial growth. Increasing population means a growing demand for agricultural products and an increasing demand for conservation of resources such as soil and water.

Income   Starting salaries for engineers with the bachelor's degree are significantly higher than starting salaries of college graduates in other fields. According to the College Placement Council, engineering graduates with a bachelor's degree and no experience averaged about $27,900 a year in private industry in 1986; those with a master's degree and no experience, $33,100 a year; and those with a Ph.D., $42,200. Starting offers for those with the bachelor's degree vary by branch.

Engineers in private industry in 1986 averaged $27,866 at the most junior level, and $79,021 at senior managerial levels. Experienced mid-level engineers with no supervisory responsibilities averaged $42,677.

Additional Sources of Information

American Society for Agricultural Engineers
2950 Niles Road
St. Joseph, MI 49085

Accreditation Board for Engineering and Technology
345 East 47th Street
New York, NY 10017

National Society of Professional Engineers
1420 King Street
Alexandria, VA 22314

American Society for Engineering Education
11 Dupont Circle
Suite 200
Washington, DC 20036

Society for Women Engineers
United Engineering Center
345 East 47th Street
New York, NY 10017

Airplane Mechanic

The Job Airplane mechanics perform scheduled maintenance, make repairs, and complete inspections required by the Federal Aviation Administration (FAA).

Many airplane mechanics specialize in either repair work or scheduled maintenance. They specialize further, and are licensed as: *powerplant mechanics,* who work on the engine; *airframe mechanics,* who work on the wings, landing gear, and structural parts of the plane; or *aircraft inspectors.* Some mechanics specialize in one type of plane or in one section of a plane such as the electrical system.

In the course of their work, airplane mechanics take engines apart; replace worn parts; use X-ray and magnetic inspection equipment; repair sheet metal surfaces; check for rust, distortion, or cracks in wings and fuselages; check electrical connections; repair and replace gauges; and then test all work after completion.

Over one-half of all airplane mechanics work for airlines; about one-third work for the federal government as civilian mechanics at military air bases. The remainder are employed in general aviation including those who work for airports in small shops and for companies that own and operate their own planes.

Mechanics employed by most major airlines belong to either the International Association of Machinists and Aerospace Workers or the Transport Workers Union of America. Some belong to the International Brotherhood of Teamsters, Chauffeurs, Warehousemen and Helpers of America.

Places of Employment and Working Conditions Airplane mechanics in general aviation work in every part of the country, as do civilians employed by the federal government at military bases. Most airline mechanics work near large cities at airports where the airlines have installations.

Mechanics usually work in hangars or other indoor areas; where repairs must be made quickly, however, they may work outdoors. Work areas are often noisy and mechanics do a lot of standing, bending, stooping, and climbing.

Qualifications, Education, and Training Physical strength, ability, good eyesight and eye-hand coordination, and mechanical aptitude are necessary.

High school courses in mathematics, physics, chemistry, and mechanical drawing are good preparation for this field. Automotive repair or other mechanical work is helpful.

5

A few airplane mechanics learn through on-the-job training, but most acquire their skills in two-year training programs at FAA-approved trade schools. Those who receive their training in the armed forces attend a shorter trade-school program to familiarize themselves with material specific to civilian aircrafts. These schools do not, however, guarantee either a job or an FAA license.

Most mechanics who work on civilian aircraft are licensed by the FAA. Applicants for all licenses must pass written and oral tests, give a practical demonstration of their ability to do the work authorized by the particular license, and fulfill the experience requirements.

At least 18 months of work experience is required for an airframe or powerplant license; 30 months for a combination airframe/powerplant license. To obtain an inspector's license, a mechanic must first hold a combination license for at least three years. Unlicensed mechanics must work under the supervision of licensed mechanics.

Potential and Advancement
There are about 110,000 airplane mechanics; another 30,000 work for aircraft manufacturers in the assembling of planes. On the whole, this job field is expected to grow steadily. In general aviation, job opportunities should be good. Although pay is often lower, many openings occur as more experienced mechanics move up to the top jobs with private companies or airlines. Competition is keen for airline jobs since the pay scale is high. Federal job opportunities will remain stable, affected primarily only by changes in defense spending.

Advancement to supervisory positions depends on experience and licenses held. Some airplane mechanics advance to executive positions or open their own repair shops.

Income
In 1986, the median annual salary of aircraft mechanics was about $26,000. Mechanics who worked on jets generally earned more than those working on other aircraft. The top 10 percent of all aircraft mechanics earned over $35,000 a year. Airline mechanics and their immediate families receive reduced fare transportation on their own and most other airlines.

Additional Sources of Information

Aviation Maintenance Foundation
P.O. Box 2826
Redmond, WA 98073

Air Transport Association of America
1709 New York Avenue, NW
Washington, DC 20006

Air Traffic Controller

The Job   The safe and efficient operation of the nation's airways and airports is the responsibility of air traffic controllers. They coordinate all flight activities to prevent accidents. Some regulate airport traffic; others regulate planes in flight between airports.

Airport traffic controllers monitor all planes in and around an airport. Planes that are not visible from the control tower are monitored on a radar screen. When the airport is busy, controllers fit the planes into a holding pattern with other planes waiting to land. The controller must keep track of all planes in the holding pattern while guiding them in for landings and instructing other planes for takeoffs.

After a plane departs the airport, the airport traffic controller notifies the appropriate *enroute controller.* There are 25 enroute control centers in the United States where enroute controllers work in teams of two or three. Each team is assigned a specific amount of airspace along one of the designated routes generally flown by all airplanes.

Before taking off, each pilot files a flight plan that is sent by teletype to the appropriate control center. When a plane enters a team's airspace, one member of the team will communicate with the pilot by radio and monitor the flight path on radar. This controller will provide information on weather, nearby planes, and other hazards and can approve and monitor such things as altitude changes.

All civilian air traffic controllers work for the Federal Aviation Administration (FAA), most of them at major airports and air traffic control centers located near large cities. Military and naval air installations use their own personnel as air traffic controllers, and many civilian controllers acquire their skills during military service.

There are very few women air traffic controllers. Aviation has always been a male-dominated field, and many air traffic controllers come from the ranks of civilian and military pilots, navigators, and controllers. As more women become pilots, they will have the required experience and background to move into jobs as air traffic controllers.

Places of Employment and Working Conditions   Air traffic controllers work at civilian and military installations throughout the country, but most of them work at main airports and air traffic control centers near large cities.

Because control towers and centers operate around the clock, seven days a week, controllers work night and weekend shifts on a rotating basis. They work under great stress because they usually have several planes under their control at one time. They must make quick decisions that affect the safety of many people.

Qualifications, Education, and Training
Potential controllers need a decisive personality, since they must make quick decisions; and they should be articulate, since instruction to pilots must be given quickly and clearly. A quick and retentive memory is a must as is the ability to work under pressure and to function calmly in an emergency.

Air traffic controller trainees are selected through the Federal Civil Service System. Applicants must be under 31 years of age, in excellent health, and have vision correctable to 20/20. They must pass a written examination that measures their ability to learn and their aptitude for the work. In addition, applicants must have three years of general work experience or four years of college or a combination of both. Applicants with experience as military controllers, pilots, or navigators may be hired without the written test.

Trainees receive 11 to 17 weeks of intensive on-the-job training combined with formal training. They learn the fundamentals of the airway system, federal aviation regulations, aircraft performance characteristics, and the use of controller equipment. Their training also includes practice on simulators at the FAA Academy in Oklahoma City.

After training, it usually takes two to three years of progressively more responsible work experience to become a fully qualified controller.

A yearly physical examination is required of all controllers, and they must pass a job performance examination twice a year.

Potential and Advancement
There are about 22,000 air traffic controllers.

Job opportunities will increase slowly during the 1990s. Competition for jobs will be stiff, however, since the number of qualified applicants is expected to exceed the number of openings. College graduates with civilian or military experience as controllers, pilots, or navigators will have the best chance of being hired.

Controllers can advance by transferring to different locations and larger airports. In installations with a number of air traffic controllers, experienced controllers can advance to supervisory positions. Some advance to management jobs in air traffic control or to administrative jobs in the FAA.

Income
Air traffic controllers who started with the FAA in 1987 earned about $18,400 (grade 7) a year. Controllers at the grade 9 level and above earn 5 percent more than other federal workers in an equivalent grade. A controller's pay is determined by both the worker's job responsibilities and the complexity

of the particular facility. Earnings are higher at facilities where traffic patterns are more complex. In 1986, controllers averaged $37,400 a year.

Depending on length of service, controllers receive 13 to 26 days of paid vacation and 13 days of paid sick leave each year; they also receive life insurance, health benefits, and a retirement program. Because of the stress of this occupation, the retirement program is more liberal than for other federal employees.

Additional Sources of Information

A pamphlet on air traffic controllers is available from the U.S. Civil Service Commission Job Information Center in your area. Ask for Announcement #418.

Personnel Operations Division
Federal Aviation Administration
800 Independence Way, SW
Washington, DC 20591

Architect

The Job An architect designs buildings and other structures—anything from a private home to a large office building or an entire city's redevelopment.

The architect must oversee all phases of the project from initial idea to completed structure. He or she must solve complex technical problems while retaining artistic design and must be able to function in a highly competitive atmosphere.

After discussing ideas, needs, and concepts with the client, the architect prepares preliminary drawings and then detailed plans for the project including the plumbing, electrical, and heating systems. He or she must specify materials that comply with local building regulations and must stay within the client's budget.

All through this process, the architect may have to make changes at the request of the client. Once plans are ready and approved, the architect may help the client select a contractor and will continue to check the work while it is in progress to ensure that all design specifications are being carried out. The architect's responsibility does not end until the structure is completed and has successfully passed all required inspections.

Architects can work in salaried positions for architectural firms or they can go into private practice. Those who decide to open their own businesses usually begin their career with a few years in salaried positions in order to accumulate experience.

Most architects are employed by architectural firms, building contractors, and community planning and redevelopment authorities. About 1,300 architects work for government agencies such as the Department of Defense, Housing and Urban Development, and the General Services Administration.

Only about 8 percent of all architects are women, but about 18 percent of the new degrees being awarded in architecture now go to women. Because this is a field where part-time practice is possible and since architects often work from their homes, the field has advantages for people with family responsibilities. There is, however, a wide salary inequality between men and women who work in architecture.

Related fields are: building contractor, urban planner.

Places of Employment and Working Conditions
Architects are employed throughout the country, in towns and cities of all sizes. A large proportion of all architectural work, however, is concentrated in Boston, Chicago, Los Angeles, New York City, Philadelphia, San Francisco, and Washington, D.C.

Architects spend many hours drawing plans and sometimes must put in overtime to meet deadlines. Once building is under way, they spend a great deal of time outdoors inspecting the progress of construction.

Qualifications, Education, and Training
Architecture requires a wide variety of technical, artistic, and social skills. Anyone planning a career in this field should be able to work independently, have a capacity for solving technical problems, and be artistic. Good business skills are also helpful.

High school students interested in architecture should take courses in mathematics, physics, and art. Summer jobs with architects or building contractors can provide useful experience.

College preparation can be either a five-year program leading to a bachelor of architecture degree or a six-year program leading to a master of architecture degree. Courses typically include architectural theory, design, graphics, engineering, urban planning, English, mathematics, chemistry, sociology, economics, and a foreign language.

Although many architects work without a license, all states require that a licensed architect take the final legal responsibility for a completed project. To qualify for the licensing examination, the applicant must have a bachelor's degree plus three years of experience in an architect's office or a master's degree plus two years of experience. Long experience (usually 12 years) may be substituted in some states, if the person can pass a preliminary qualifying test.

Potential and Advancement   There are approximately 84,000 architects in the country at present, most of them in large cities. Prospects for employment in architecture depend upon the number of degrees being granted and the rise and fall of the building market. With an increase in schools that grant architectural degrees and a growing interest in more efficient housing and public construction, jobs will be available, but competition is expected to be keen. Most openings will occur in architectural firms, but some jobs will also be available in government agencies and in colleges and universities.

New graduates usually begin as junior drafters and work their way up to increased responsibility. They may be promoted to chief or senior drafter or put in charge of one phase of a large project such as design, specification writing, or construction supervision.

Income   The median annual earnings for salaried architects who worked full time were about $30,000 in 1986. The middle 50 percent earned between $21,700 and $37,600. The top 10 percent earned more than $51,100 and the lowest 10 percent, less than $16,200.

Architects who are partners in well-established architectural firms or solo practitioners generally earn much more than their salaried employees, but their income may fluctuate due to changing business conditions. Architects may have difficulty getting established in their own practices and may go through a period when their expenses are greater than their income.

In 1986, the average salary for architects working in the federal government was about $36,500.

Additional Sources of Information

The American Institute of Architecture
1735 New York Avenue, NW
Washington, DC 20006

The Association of Collegiate Schools of Architecture, Inc.
1735 New York Avenue, NW
Washington, DC 20006

The National Council of Architectural Registration Boards
1735 New York Avenue, NW
Suite 700
Washington, DC 20006

Biochemist

The Job Biochemists study the chemical composition and behavior of living things and the effects of food, drugs, hormones, and other chemicals on various organisms. Their work is essential to a better understanding of health, growth, reproduction, and heredity in human beings and to progress in the fields of medicine, nutrition, and agriculture.

Most biochemists are involved in basic research; those engaged in applied research use the results of basic research to solve practical problems. For example, basic research into how an organism forms a hormone has been used to synthesize and produce hormones on a mass scale.

Laboratory research can involve weighing, filtering, distilling, and culturing specimens or the operation of electron microscopes and centrifuges. Biochemists sometimes design new laboratory apparatus or develop new techniques to carry out specific research projects.

About half of all biochemists are employed in colleges and universities, where they combine their research work with teaching positions. Other job opportunity fields for biochemists are the drug, insecticide, and cosmetic industries, where about one-fourth work, and nonprofit research foundations and government agencies in the areas of health and agriculture.

Places of Employment and Working Conditions Biochemists are employed in all regions of the country, mainly in areas where chemical, food, and drug industries and colleges and universities are located.

Laboratory work can involve the handling of dangerous or unpleasant substances. Biochemists involved in research projects may work irregular or extended hours during certain phases of a project.

Qualifications, Education, and Training Keen powers of observation, a curious mind, patience and perseverance, mechanical aptitude, and good communication skills are among the abilities necessary for the biochemist. Anyone planning a career in this field should be able to work either independently or as part of a team.

An advanced degree is the minimum required, even for many beginning jobs in this field. The prospective biochemist should begin with an undergraduate degree in chemistry, biology, or biochemistry, which will also involve courses in mathematics and physics.

About 150 colleges and universities offer graduate degrees in biochemistry. These programs require research as well as advanced science courses, usually in some specialized area. The student should choose a graduate school carefully because certain types of research facilities exist only at certain schools.

A Ph.D. degree is almost mandatory for anyone who hopes to do significant biochemical research or advance to management and administrative levels. This degree requires extensive original research and the writing of a thesis.

Potential and Advancement There are presently about 16,000 biochemists in the United States. Job prospects in the next ten years are expected to be very good, as a result of efforts to cure major diseases, concern for the safety of food and drug products, and public awareness of environmental and pollution problems. Biochemists will also be needed in the drug manufacturing industry, in hospitals and health centers, in colleges and universities, and in federal regulatory agencies.

Beginners in biochemistry jobs usually start work as technicians or assistants doing testing and analysis. They may advance, through increased experience and education, to positions that involve planning and supervising research. Positions in administration and management can be achieved by those with experience and an advanced degree, but many prefer to remain in the laboratory— doing basic biochemical research.

Income According to the College Placement Council, beginning salary offers in private industry in 1986 averaged $19,000 a year for bachelor's degree recipients in biological science.

In the federal government in 1987, biological scientists having a bachelor's degree could begin at $14,822 or $18,358 a year, depending on their college records. Those having the master's degree could start at $18,358 or $22,458, depending on their academic records or work experience; those having the Ph.D. degree could begin at $27,172 or $32,567 a year. Biological scientists in the federal government averaged $37,200 a year in 1986.

Additional Sources of Information

American Society of Biochemistry and Molecular Biology
9650 Rockville Pike
Bethesda, MD 20014

Biomedical Engineer

The Job   Biomedical engineers apply engineering principles to medical and health-related problems.

Most engineers in this field are involved in research. They work with life scientists, chemists, and members of the medical profession to design and develop medical devices such as artificial hearts, pacemakers, dialysis machines, and lasers for surgery. Others work for private industry in the development, design, and sales of medical instruments and devices.

Biomedical engineers with computer expertise adapt computers to medical needs and design and build systems to modernize laboratory and clinical procedures. Some work for the National Aeronautics and Space Administration developing life support and medical monitoring systems for astronauts.

Places of Employment and Working Conditions   Some phases of this work may be unpleasant when one is working with certain illnesses or medical conditions.

Qualifications, Education, and Training   The ability to think analytically, a capacity for details, and the ability to work as part of a team are all necessary. Good communication skills are important.

Mathematics and the sciences must be emphasized in high school. A bachelor's degree in engineering is the minimum requirement in this field. In a typical curriculum, the first two years are spent in the study of basic sciences such as physics and chemistry and mathematics, introductory engineering, and some liberal arts courses. The remaining years are usually devoted to specialized engineering courses. For this field that means a sound background in mechanical, electrical, industrial, or chemical engineering plus additional specialized biomedical training.

Engineering programs can last from four to six years. Those that require five or six years to complete may award a master's degree or may provide a cooperative plan of study plus practical work experience with a nearby industry.

All states require licensing of engineers whose work may affect life, health, or property or who offer their services to the public. Those who are licensed, about one-third of all engineers, are called registered engineers. Requirements for licensing include graduation from an accredited engineering school, four years of experience, and an examination.

Potential and Advancement   There are only about 4,000 biomedical engineers. Substantial growth is expected, but, since the field is relatively small, few actual job openings will occur. Those with advance degrees will have the best job opportunities.

Income   Starting salaries in private industry average $33,500 with a master's degree and $36,500 or more with a Ph.D.

The federal government pays beginners $17,947 to $26,763, depending on degree and experience. Average salary for experienced engineers, federally employed, is about $29,000.

Experienced biomedical engineers average $34,500 in private industry; $23,000 to $43,000 for nine-month faculty positions in colleges and universities.

Additional Sources of Information

Alliance for Engineering in Medicine and Biology
1101 Connecticut Avenue, NW
Suite 700
Washington, DC 20036

Biomedical Engineering Society
P.O. Box 2399
Culver City, CA 90230

Engineers' Council for Professional Development
345 East 47th Street
New York, NY 10017

National Society of Professional Engineers
1420 King Street
Alexandria, VA 22314

American Society for Engineering Education
11 Dupont Circle, NW
Suite 200
Washington, DC 20036

Society of Women Engineers
United Engineering Center
345 East 47th Street
New York, NY 10017

Broadcasting Technician

The Job The operation and maintenance of the electronic equipment used to record and transmit radio and television programs is the responsibility of broadcasting technicians, also called broadcasting engineers.

In small stations, broadcasting technicians perform a variety of duties. In large stations and in networks, technicians are more specialized. They may perform any or all of the following functions.

Transmitter technicians monitor and log (keep records of) outgoing signals and are responsible for transmitter operation. *Maintenance technicians* set up, maintain, and repair the broadcasting equipment. *Audio control technicians* regulate sound; *video control technicians* regulate the quality of television pictures; and *lighting technicians* direct the lighting. *Recording technicians* operate and maintain sound recording equipment, while *video recording technicians* operate and maintain video tape recording equipment. When programs originate outside of a radio or television station, *field technicians* set up and operate the broadcasting equipment.

Radio stations usually employ only a few broadcasting technicians, 3 to 10, depending on the size and broadcasting schedule of the station. Television broadcasting is more complex, and television stations usually employ between 10 and 30 technicians in addition to supervisory personnel.

Related jobs are: communications technician, television and radio service technician.

Places of Employment and Working Conditions
Broadcasting technicians are employed in all areas of the United States, especially in large metropolitan areas. The highest paid and most specialized jobs are in Los Angeles, New York City, and Washington, D.C., where most network programs originate.

In large stations, broadcasting technicians work a 37- to 40-hour week. In smaller stations, the workweek is usually longer. In stations that broadcast 24 hours a day, seven days a week, some weekend, evening, and holiday work is necessary. Network technicians covering an important event often have to work continuously and under great pressure until the event is over.

Qualifications, Education, and Training
Manual dexterity, good eyesight and hearing, reliability, and the ability to work as part of a team are all requisites for anyone interested in this field.

High school should include algebra, trigonometry, physics, and electrical shop. Electronics courses can also provide valuable background.

Many technical schools and colleges offer special courses for broadcasting technicians. These courses are designed to prepare the student to take the Federal Communications Commission (FCC) licensing examinations.

The FCC issues a Third Class operator license and a First Class radio-telephone operator license. Applicants for either license must pass a series of examinations. Anyone who operates a transmitter in a television station must have a license; the chief engineer at any broadcasting station must have one as well. Some radio and television stations require all technicians to have at least a Third Class license.

A college degree in engineering is becoming necessary for many supervisory and executive positions in broadcasting.

Potential and Advancement   There are about 27,000 broadcasting technicians. Any job openings that are likely to occur will be to replace technicians who retire or transfer to other occupations. Although the growth of cable television will provide some new jobs, this could be offset by the increasing use of automated equipment for some of the jobs normally handled by broadcasting technicians.

Beginners will face the most competition for available jobs, and for them the best opportunities will be in smaller cities.

Broadcasting technicians can advance to supervisory positions such as chief engineer. Top-level technical positions such as director of engineering usually require a college degree.

Income   According to a survey conducted by the National Association of Broadcasters, average earnings for technicians at radio stations were $20,000 a year in 1986; in television, about $22,000. Television stations usually pay higher salaries than radio stations because television work is generally more complex. Technicians employed by educational broadcasting stations generally earn less than those who work for commercial stations.

Additional Sources of Information

National Association of Broadcasters
1771 N Street, NW
Washington, DC 20036

Corporation for Public Broadcasting
1111 16th Street
Washington, DC 20036

Federal Communications Commission
Washington, DC 20554

Business Machine Service Technician

The Job   Maintenance and repair of business and office machines is the work of business machine service technicians. About 80 percent of these technicians work for business machine manufacturers and dealers or repair shops; the remainder work for large organizations that have enough machines to employ an in-house, full-time technician.

The majority of business machine service technicians work on typewriters, calculators and adding machines, and copiers and duplicating equipment. A few repair and service dictating machines; the remainder service accounting-bookkeeping machines, cash registers, and postage and mailing equipment.

Technicians usually specialize in one type of business machine, such as typewriters or copiers. Those who work for a manufacturer or dealer probably service only the brand produced or sold by their employer.

Related jobs are: appliance repairer, computer service technician, communications technician, television and radio service technician.

Places of Employment and Working Conditions   Business machine service technicians work in communities of all sizes throughout the country. Even small communities have at least one repair shop or self-employed technician.

Servicing business machines is cleaner work than most mechanical jobs, and business machine service technicians usually wear business clothes. There are no slow periods since business machines must be serviced regardless of slack economic periods.

Qualifications, Education, and Training   Mechanical ability, manual dexterity, good eyesight and hearing, and the ability to work without supervision are required for this work. Since these technicians work directly with the customer, they must also be pleasant and tactful.

High school classes in electrical shop, mechanical drawing, mathematics, and physics are helpful.

There are no specific educational requirements for this field, but many employers prefer some technical training in electricity or electronics. Courses are available at trade and technical schools and junior and community colleges. Training received in the armed forces is also valuable.

Trainees who are hired by a manufacturer or dealer attend a training program sponsored by the manufacturer. Such programs last from several weeks to several months and are followed by one to three years of on-the-job training. Training offered by independent repair shops is less formal but basically the same.

All business machine service technicians keep up with technological changes by attending frequent training seminars sponsored by manufacturers when new machines are developed. Many companies also provide tuition assistance for technicians who take additional work-related courses in colleges or technical schools.

Potential and Advancement   There are about 58,000 business machine service technicians, and the field is expanding rapidly. Job opportunities will be especially good for those with some training in electronics. Since electronic business machines are becoming more and more popular, in a few years, an electronics background will be essential for all business machine service technicians.

Advancement to positions such as service manager or supervisor is possible for experienced technicians. Some open their own repair business or go into business machine sales.

Income   Median annual earnings of full-time office machine and cash register servicers were about $19,600 in 1986; the middle 50 percent earned between $14,900 and $25,900. Ten percent earned less than $11,400, and 10 percent earned more than $31,800.

Technicians who service electronic business machines and complex copiers earn the highest wages.

Additional Sources of Information

Local offices of firms that sell and service business machines can provide information on job opportunities and training.

Ceramic Engineer

The Job   Ceramic engineers work not only with ceramics (as in pottery) but with all nonmetallic, inorganic materials that require high temperatures in their processing. Thus these engineers work on such diverse products as glassware, heat-resistant materials for furnaces, electronic components, and nuclear reactors. They also design and supervise construction of plants and equipment used in the manufacture of these products.

Ceramic engineers normally specialize in one or more ceramic products— whiteware (porcelain and china or high-voltage electrical insulators); structural materials such as brick and tile; electronic ceramics, glass, or fuel elements for atomic energy, to name a few. Most are employed in the stone, clay, and glass industries. Others work in industries that use ceramic products including the iron and steel, electrical equipment, aerospace, and chemical industries.

Places of Employment and Working Conditions   Ceramic engineers are employed in all areas of the country. Their work locations vary from laboratories to factory production areas, depending on the product and the industry.

Qualifications, Education, and Training   The ability to think analytically, a capacity for details, and the ability to work as part of a team are all necessary. Good communication skills are important for the ceramic engineer.

Mathematics and the sciences must be emphasized in high school.

A bachelor's degree in engineering is the minimum requirement in this field. In a typical curriculum, the first two years are spent in the study of basic sciences such as physics and chemistry and mathematics, introductory engineering, and some liberal arts courses. The remaining years are usually devoted to specialized engineering courses. Engineering programs can last from four to six years. Those requiring five or six years to complete may award a master's degree or may provide a cooperative plan of study plus practical work experience with a nearby industry.

Because of rapid changes in technology, many ceramic engineers continue their education throughout their careers. A graduate degree is necessary for most teaching and research positions and for many management jobs. Some persons obtain graduate degrees in business administration.

Engineering graduates usually work under the supervision of an experienced engineer or in a company training program until they become acquainted with the requirements of a particular company.

All states require licensing of engineers whose work may affect life, health, or property or who offer their services to the public. Those who are licensed, about one-third of all engineers, are called registered engineers. Requirements include graduation from an accredited engineering school, four years of experience, and an examination.

Potential and Advancement   There are about 15,000 ceramic engineers, and job opportunities in this field are expected to increase substantially into the 1990s. Nuclear energy, electronics, defense, medical science, pollution control, energy, and conservation will all offer increasing job opportunities for ceramic engineers.

Income   Starting salaries for engineers with the bachelor's degree are significantly higher than starting salaries of college graduates in other fields. According to the College Placement Council, engineering graduates with a bachelor's degree and no experience averaged about $27,900 a year in private industry in 1986; those with a master's degree and no experience, $33,100 a year; and those with a Ph.D., $42,200. Starting offers for those with the bachelor's degree vary by branch.

Additional Sources of Information

American Ceramic Society
757 Brooksedge Plaza Drive
Westerville, OH 43081

Accreditation Board for Engineering and Technology
345 East 47th Street
New York, NY 10017

National Society of Professional Engineers
1420 King Street
Alexandria, VA 22314

American Society for Engineering Education
11 Dupont Circle
Suite 200
Washington, DC 20036

Society of Women Engineers
United Engineering Center
345 East 47th Street
New York, NY 10017

Chemical Engineer

The Job   The duties of chemical engineers entail a working knowledge of chemistry, physics, and mechanical and electrical engineering.

Chemical engineers design chemical plants, manufacturing equipment, and production methods; they develop processes for such things as removing chemical contaminants from waste materials.

This is one of the most complex and diverse areas of engineering. Chemical engineers often specialize in a particular operation such as oxidation or polymerization. Others specialize in plastics or rubber or in a field such as pollution control.

Most chemical engineers work in manufacturing firms primarily in chemicals, petroleum, and related industries. A number of them work in the nuclear energy field.

Places of Employment and Working Conditions   Chemical engineers may be subject to hazards that occur when working with dangerous chemicals.

Qualifications, Education, and Training   The ability to think analytically, a capacity for details, and the ability to work as part of a team are all necessary. Good communication skills are important for anyone who holds chemical engineering as a career goal.

Mathematics and the sciences should be emphasized as much as possible in high school.

A bachelor's degree in engineering is the minimum requirement in this field. In a typical curriculum, the first two years are spent in the study of basic sciences such as physics and chemistry and mathematics, introductory engineering, and some liberal arts courses. The remaining years are usually devoted to specialized engineering courses. Engineering programs can last from four to six years. Those requiring five or six years to complete may award a master's degree or may provide a plan of study along with work experience with a nearby industry.

Because of rapid changes in technology, many engineers continue their education throughout their careers. A graduate degree is necessary for most teaching and research positions and for many management jobs. Some chemical engineers obtain graduate degrees in business administration.

Graduates usually work under the supervision of an experienced chemical engineer or in a company training program until they become acquainted with the requirements of a particular company.

All states require licensing of engineers whose work may affect life, health, or property or who offer their services to the public. Those who are licensed, about one-third of all engineers, are called registered engineers. Requirements for licensing include graduation from an accredited engineering school, four years of experience, and an examination.

Potential and Advancement   There are about 52,000 chemical engineers. Job opportunities should be good through the 1990s, especially in the fields of pollution control and environmental protection, development of synthetic fuels, and nuclear energy.

Income   Starting salaries for engineers with the bachelor's degree are significantly higher than starting salaries of college graduates in other fields. According to the College Placement Council, engineering graduates with a bachelor's degree and no experience averaged about $27,900 a year in private industry in 1986; those with a master's degree and no experience, $33,100 a year; and those with a Ph.D., $42,200. Starting offers for those with the bachelor's degree vary by branch. Engineers in private industry in 1986 averaged $27,866 at the most junior level, and $79,021 at senior managerial levels. Experienced mid-level engineers with no supervisory responsibilities averaged $42,677.

Additional Sources of Information

American Institute of Chemical Engineers
345 East 47th Street
New York, NY 10017

Accreditation Board for Engineering and Technology
345 East 47th Street
New York, NY 10017

National Society of Professional Engineers
1420 King Street
Alexandria, VA 22314

American Society for Engineering Education
11 Dupont Circle
Suite 200
Washington, DC 20036

Society of Women Engineers
United Engineering Center
345 East 47th Street
New York, NY 10017

Chemist

The Job   Chemists perform laboratory research to gain new knowledge about the substances that make up our world. Knowledge gained in basic research is then put to practical use and applied to the development of new products. For example, basic research on the uniting of small molecules to form larger ones (polymerization) led to the development of products made from synthetic rubber and plastic.

Many chemists work in industrial production and inspection, where they must coordinate their efforts with a manufacturing operation. They give directions for the carrying out of a manufacturing process and then take periodic samples to check that process. Others work as marketing sales representatives because of the technical knowledge needed to market certain products. Chemists also work as college teachers and researchers and as consultants.

Chemists often specialize in one of the subfields of chemistry. *Analytical chemists* study the structure, composition, and natures of substances. *Organic chemists* study all elements made from carbon compounds, which include vast areas of modern industry. The development of plastics and many other synthetics is the result of the work of organic chemists. *Inorganic chemists* study compounds other than carbon and are involved in the development of such things as solid-state electronic components. *Physical chemists* study energy transformation and are engaged in finding new and better energy sources.

More than half of all chemists work in the chemical, food, petroleum, paper, electrical, and scientific instrument industries. About 25,000 work in colleges and universities and another 25,000 for government agencies, primarily in health and agriculture.

About 12 percent of all chemists are women.

Related jobs are: biochemist, food scientist, and life scientist.

Places of Employment and Working Conditions   Although chemists work in all parts of the country, the largest concentrations are in New York, New Jersey, California, Pennsylvania, Ohio, and Illinois.

Chemists usually work in modern facilities in laboratories, classrooms, and offices. In certain industries, hazards are present in the handling of explosive or otherwise dangerous materials, but safety regulations in these industries are very strict.

Qualifications, Education, and Training

The student who plans a career as a chemist should enjoy performing experiments and building things and should have a genuine liking for math and science. A wide range of abilities is necessary, including perseverance, concentration on detail, good eye-hand coordination, and the ability to work independently.

High school students looking forward to a career in chemistry should take as many math and science courses as possible and should develop good laboratory skills. Foreign language courses can also prove valuable.

Over 1,000 colleges and universities offer a bachelor's degree in chemistry. Courses include analytical, organic and inorganic, and physical chemistry, as well as mathematics and physics.

A master's degree in chemistry, usually requiring extensive, independent research, is offered by about 350 colleges and universities. Original research is required for a Ph.D. degree.

Potential and Advancement

About 86,000 people are presently employed as chemists. The outlook for employment is good primarily because of the development of new products by private industry. In addition, problems of pollution, energy, and health care must be addressed by chemists in both government agencies and private industry. Employment of chemists in crime detection work is also expected to increase on local, state, and federal levels.

Little growth is expected in college and university positions, and competition for existing teaching jobs is expected to be very strong. Candidates for advanced degrees may secure teaching or research positions while completing their studies, but these positions are usually at the assistant or instructor level.

In all areas, advanced degrees will continue to be the key to administrative and managerial positions. College professors, chemists doing basic research, and those employed in the top administrative positions in both industry and teaching will need a Ph.D. degree to achieve these levels.

Income

According to the College Placement Council, chemists with a bachelor's degree were offered starting salaries averaging $23,400 a year in 1986; those with a master's degree, $28,000; and those with a Ph.D., $36,400.

According to the American Chemical Society, median salaries of their members with a bachelor's degree were $33,000 a year in 1986; with a master's degree, $37,900; with a Ph.D., $47,800.

In a Bureau of Labor Statistics survey, chemists in private industry averaged $22,500 a year in 1986 at the most junior level, and $74,600 at senior supervisory levels. Experienced midlevel chemists with no supervisory responsibilities averaged $41,500.

Additional Sources of Information

American Chemical Society
1155 16th Street, NW
Washington, DC 20036

Chemical Manufacturers Association
2501 M Street, NW
Washington, DC 20037

Interagency Board of U.S. Civil Service Examiners for Washington, DC
1900 E Street, NW
Washington, DC 20415

Civil Engineer

The Job   This is the oldest branch of the engineering profession. Civil engineers design and supervise construction of buildings, roads, harbors, airports, dams, tunnels and bridges, and water supply and sewage systems.

Specialties within civil engineering include structural, hydraulic, environmental (sanitary), transportation, geotechnical, and soil mechanics. Many civil engineers are in supervisory or administrative positions. They may supervise a construction site or administer a large municipal project such as highway or airport construction.

Most civil engineers work for construction companies or for federal, state, and local government agencies. Others work for public utilities, railroads, architectural firms, and engineering consulting firms. A number of them work in the nuclear energy field.

Places of Employment and Working Conditions   Civil engineers work in all parts of the country, usually in or near major industrial and commercial centers. Some work for American firms in foreign countries.

A great deal of the civil engineer's time is spent outdoors. They sometimes work in remote areas and may have to move from place to place as they work on different projects.

Qualifications, Education, and Training

The ability to think analytically, a capacity for detail, and the ability to work as part of a team are all necessary. Good communication skills are important.

Mathematics and the sciences must be emphasized in high school.

A bachelor's degree in engineering is the minimum requirement in this field. In a typical curriculum, the first two years are spent in the study of basic sciences such as physics and chemistry and mathematics, introductory engineering, and some liberal arts courses. The remaining years are usually devoted to specialized engineering courses. Engineering programs can last from four to six years. Those requiring five or six years to complete may award a master's degree or may provide a cooperative plan of study plus practical work experience in a nearby industry.

Because of rapid changes in technology, many engineers continue their education throughout their careers. A graduate degree is necessary for most teaching and research positions and for many management jobs. Some persons obtain graduate degrees in business administration.

Engineering graduates usually work under the supervision of an experienced engineer or in a company training program until they become acquainted with the requirements of a particular company or industry.

All states require licensing of engineers whose work may affect life, health, or property or who offer their services to the public. Those who are licensed, about one-third of all engineers, are called registered engineers. Requirements include graduation from an accredited engineering school, four years of experience, and a written examination.

Potential and Advancement

There are about 199,000 civil engineers. Job opportunities in this field will increase somewhat because population growth will create an increasing demand for housing, transportation, power generating plants, and other energy sources.

Income

Starting salaries for engineers with the bachelor's degree are significantly higher than starting salaries of college graduates in other fields. According to the College Placement Council, engineering graduates with a bachelor's degree and no experience averaged about $27,900 a year in private industry in 1986; those with a master's degree and no experience, $33,100 a year; and those with a Ph.D., $42,200. Starting offers for those with the bachelor's degree vary by branch. Engineers in private industry in 1986 averaged

,866 at the most junior level, and $79,021 at senior managerial levels. Expe-
.enced mid-level engineers with no supervisory responsibilities averaged
$42,677.

Additional Sources of Information

American Society of Civil Engineers
345 East 47th Street
New York, NY 10017

Accreditation Board for Engineering and Technology
345 East 47th Street
New York, NY 10017

National Society of Professional Engineers
1420 King Street
Alexandria, VA 22314

American Society for Engineering Education
11 Dupont Circle
Suite 200
Washington, DC 20036

Society of Women Engineers
United Engineering Center
345 East 47th Street
New York, NY 10017

Communications Technician

The Job   The installation, maintenance, and repair of communications
equipment are the responsibility of communications technicians. This equipment includes telephone, telegraph, wireless, and cable equipment as well as
radio, television, and radar broadcasting equipment. (Broadcasting Technicians,
who are equipment operators, are covered in another job description under that
title.)

Communications technicians are employed by communications systems, manufacturers of communications equipment, airlines, police and fire departments, government agencies, and radio and television studios.

Communications technicians have various duties and specialties:

Central office equipment installers handle the installation of switchboards, dialing equipment, and other equipment in the central office of a telephone company. *Station installers* and *repairpersons* install and service telephone equipment in homes, offices, businesses, and telephone booths and maintain outside facilities. *PBX installers* and *repairpersons* work on private switchboard equipment. *Linepersons* and *cable splicers* install and maintain aerial and underground wires and cables.

Radio and telephone technical operators set up and adjust overseas radio-telephone communication equipment. They contact foreign terminals and make mutually agreed-upon adjustments in transmitting power, frequency, and speech levels.

In radio and television studios, a *construction technician* installs broadcasting equipment, assembles and wires units of technical equipment, and assists in testing the equipment.

Radar technicians install and service radar equipment.

Related jobs include: broadcasting technician, television and radio service technician.

Places of Employment and Working Conditions
Positions for communications technicians are available throughout the United States and in many locations overseas.

Technicians usually work a 40-hour week. Emergency situations caused by bad weather or such incidents as fires or accidents may require periods of long or irregular work hours. Communications technicians are also subject to injury from electrical shocks and falls.

Qualifications, Education, and Training
Mechanical aptitude, manual dexterity, normal eyesight and hearing, physical stamina, and the ability to work as part of a team are necessary.

High school should include courses in mathematics, physics, and electrical shop. Hobbies that deal with electronics and communication equipment are helpful.

Some companies, especially telephone companies, provide their own training programs and require only a high school diploma. Other employers prefer a year or two of training at a technical or trade school or a junior or community college. Some communications equipment manufacturers also offer training courses.

Training received in communications operation and service in the armed forces is also very valuable in civilian jobs. Correspondence courses are also available.

Because of rapid technological changes in communications equipment, technicians usually take frequent company-sponsored courses to keep themselves up-to-date. Many organizations provide tuition assistance for technicians who take work-related courses at technical schools and colleges.

Some technicians in this field are required to have a Federal Communications Commission radio operator's license. Most technical courses prepare the student for the appropriate licensing examination.

Potential and Advancement   The rapidly expanding demand for communications systems and equipment of all types makes this an excellent employment field. In many areas of the country, qualified technicians are in short supply, especially in areas experiencing rapid population growth.

Experienced communications technicians can advance to supervisory positions. Advanced technical training is necessary for some positions.

Income   Telephone installers and other telephone technicians earn between $348 and $793 a week, depending on local union wage scales.

Earnings for communications technicians in other fields vary so greatly, depending on size and location of employer, that average figures are not available.

Additional Sources of Information

Local telephone and telegraph companies and radio and television stations can provide information on job requirements.

Computer Programmer

The Job   Computer programmers write detailed instructions, called programs, that list the orderly steps a computer must follow to solve a problem. Once programming is completed, the programmer runs a sample of the data to make sure the program is correct and will produce the desired information. This is called "debugging." If there are any errors, the program must be changed and rechecked until it produces the correct results. The final step is the preparation of an instruction sheet for the computer operator who will run the program.

A simple program can be written and debugged in a few days. Those that use many data files or complex mathematical formulas may require a year or more of work. On such large projects, several programmers work together under the supervision of an experienced programmer.

Programmers usually work from problem descriptions prepared by *systems analysts* who have examined the problem and determined the next steps necessary to solve it. In organizations that do not employ systems analysts, employees called *programmer-analysts* handle both functions. An *applications programmer* then writes detailed instructions for programming the data. Application programmers usually specialize in business or scientific work.

A *systems programmer* is a specialist who maintains the general instructions (software) that control the operation of the entire computer system.

Beginners in this field spend several months working under supervision before they begin to handle all aspects of the job.

Most programmers are employed by manufacturing firms, banks, insurance companies, data processing services, utilities, and government agencies. Systems programmers usually work in research organizations, computer manufacturing firms, and large computer centers.

About 22 percent of all computer programmers are women.

Places of Employment and Working Conditions   Programmers are employed in all areas of the country.

Most programmers work a 40-hour week, but their hours are not always 9:00 to 5:00. They may occasionally work on weekends or at other odd hours to have access to the computer when it is not needed for scheduled work.

Qualifications, Education, and Training   Patience, persistence, and accuracy are necessary characteristics for a programmer. Ingenuity, imagination, and the ability to think logically are also important.

High school experience also should include as many mathematics courses as possible.

There are no standard training requirements for programmers. Depending on the work to be done, an employer may require only some special courses in computer programming, or a college education, or a graduate degree in computer science, mathematics, or engineering.

Computer programming courses are offered by vocational and technical schools, colleges and universities, and junior colleges. Homestudy courses are also available, and a few high schools offer some training in programming.

Scientific organizations require college training; some require advanced degrees in computer science, mathematics, engineering, or the physical sciences.

Because of rapidly changing technologies, programmers take periodic training courses offered by employers, software vendors, and computer manufacturers. Like physicians, they must keep constantly abreast of the latest developments in their field. These courses also aid in advancement and promotion.

Potential and Advancement

There are about 479,000 computer programmers. This is a rapidly growing field because of the expanding use of computers. Simpler programming needs will be increasingly handled by improved software so that programmers with only the most basic training will not find as many job openings as in the recent past. A strong demand will continue, however, for college graduates with a major in computer science or a related field. Graduates of two-year programs should find ample job openings in business applications.

There are many opportunities for advancement in this field. In large organizations, programmers may be promoted to lead programmers with supervisory responsibilities. Both applications programmers and systems programmers can be promoted to systems analyst positions.

Income

Median earnings of programmers who worked full time in 1986 were about $27,000 a year. The middle 50 percent earned between $20,700 and $33,900 annually. The lowest 10 percent earned less than $15,700, and the highest 10 percent more than $43,100.

In the federal government, the entrance salary for programmers with a college degree was about $14,800 a year in 1987.

Programmers working in the West and Northeast earned somewhat more than those working in the South and Midwest. Salaries tend to be highest in mining and public utilities and lowest in finance, insurance, and real estate. On average, systems programmers earn more than applications programmers.

Additional Sources of Information

Data Processing Management Association
505 Busse Highway
Park Ridge, IL 60068

American Federation of Information Processing Societies
1899 Preston White Drive
Reston, VA 22091

Association for Computing Machinery
11 West 42nd Street
New York, NY 10036

Computer Service Technician

The Job   Computer systems perform a wide variety of tasks in business and industry. Keeping the systems in working order is the responsibility of computer service technicians.

Computer service technicians not only do repair work but also provide regular scheduled maintenance checks to prevent emergency breakdowns of equipment. Some computer technicians install new equipment, while others design and develop maintenance and repair schedules and manuals. Some technicians specialize in a particular computer model or system or in a certain type of repair.

Most computer service technicians are employed by the manufacturers of computer equipment or by firms that contract to provide maintenance service to a manufacturer's customers. A few are employed directly by organizations that have large computer installations.

Related jobs are: appliance repairer, business machine service technician, communications technician, television and radio service technician.

Places of Employment and Working Conditions   Computer service technicians work out of regional offices located in major urban areas. About one-quarter of all technicians work in Chicago, Los Angeles, New York City, Philadelphia, and Washington, D.C.

The normal workweek is 40 hours, but large amounts of overtime can be standard. Many service technicians work rotating shifts or are on call 24 hours a day because many businesses run their computers around the clock.

Qualifications, Education, and Training   Mechanical aptitude, manual dexterity, good eyesight and color vision, normal hearing, patience, and the ability to work without supervision are necessary. Because technicians work directly with customers, they must get along well with people.

A high school student interested in this field should take courses in mathematics, physics, and electrical shop. Hobbies that involve electronics, such as ham radio operation or building stereo equipment, are helpful.

Employers usually prefer to hire trainees with one or two years of technical training in electronics or electrical engineering. Technical and vocational schools, junior colleges, and the armed forces provide this training.

Trainers usually attend a company training center for three to six months and then complete six months to two years of on-the-job training. Because of constant technological changes in the field, all technicians normally take periodic training courses as new equipment is developed.

Experienced technicians may take advanced courses for specialization in particular systems or repairs. Some technicians study computer programming and systems analysis to broaden their general knowledge of computer operation.

Potential and Advancement   There are about 69,000 computer service technicians, and the field is expanding rapidly. Since most people in the computer field are relatively young, few job openings will occur because of death or retirement; almost all openings will result from the rising demand for computers.

Experienced technicians may advance to supervisory positions or may become specialists or troubleshooters who diagnose difficult problems. Some transfer into sales.

Income   Median annual earnings of full-time computer service technicians were about $26,700 in 1986. The middle 50 percent earned between $21,300 and $34,400. The lowest 10 percent earned less than $15,800 a year. Many of these probably were trainees. The top 10 percent of technicians earned over $40,800 a year.

Additional Sources of Information

Manufacturers of computers can provide information on job opportunities and training programs.

Criminologist

The Job   The field of criminology broadly covers all those who work in law enforcement, criminal courts, prisons and other correctional institutions, and counseling and rehabilitation programs for offenders. Many jobs in these categories are covered elsewhere in this book. This job description, however, focuses on the term "criminologist" as it applies to those who are involved in the scientific investigation of crime through analysis of evidence.

The scientific gathering, investigation, and evaluation of evidence is known as criminalistics, and those who work in this field are called *forensic scientists.* These technical experts, including specially trained police officers and detectives, carefully search victims, vehicles, and scenes of crimes. They take photographs, make sketches, lift fingerprints, make casts of footprints and tire tracks, and gather samples of any other relevant materials.

Once the evidence has been gathered, scientists and technicians trained in various natural sciences analyze it along with reports from medical examiners and pathologists. Other specialists interview victims to prepare composite pictures or psychological profiles of the criminal. Those who specialize in firearms and ballistics conduct tests that identify weapons used in specific crimes.

Forensic specialists also include handwriting experts, fingerprint and voiceprint specialists, polygraphy (lie detector) examiners, and odontologists (teeth and bite-mark specialists).

Almost all the people in this field work for federal, state, or local law enforcement and investigative agencies. Municipal and state police departments all have investigative responsibilities that include the processing of evidence. Some employ civilian scientists and technicians, but many utilize specially trained police officers in police crime laboratories.

The federal government employs forensic scientists in a number of agencies including the Federal Bureau of Investigation and the Secret Service.

Related jobs are: chemist, medical laboratory technologist, biochemist, police officer.

Places of Employment and Working Conditions   Forensic
scientists may be on call at all hours and may be required to work out-of-doors or in unpleasant conditions when gathering evidence.

Qualifications, Education, and Training   Personal traits of cu-
riosity, ability to work with detail, patience, and good eyesight and color vision are necessary.

High school should include mathematics and science courses.

College training depends on the specialty field selected. A degree in chemistry, biology, electronics, or whatever related field is appropriate should be obtained. Course work in forensic science is offered by some colleges and by law enforcement training programs and police departments.

Potential and Advancement The increasing sophistication of crime detection and investigative procedures will mean growth of job opportunities for those trained in the scientific methods necessary. Growth in population and the resulting increase in crime also will increase the demand for qualified forensic scientists.

Income According to a 1985 survey by the National Science Foundation, the median annual salary of sociologists and anthropologists combined was $37,200. For those in educational institutions, it was $37,000, and in business and industry, $45,000.

Additional Sources of Information

Federal Bureau of Investigation
U.S. Department of Justice
Washington, DC 20535

American Society of Criminology
1314 Kinnear Road
Columbus, OH 43212

Drafter

The Job Drafters prepare detailed drawings from rough sketches, specifications, and calculations made by engineers, architects, designers, and scientists. Work completed by a drafter usually includes a detailed view of the object from all sizes, specifications for materials to be used, and procedures to be followed. Any other information necessary to carry out the job is also included by the drafter.

Drafters usually specialize in a particular field, such as mechanical, electronic, structural, architectural, electrical, or aeronautical drafting. They are classified according to the work they do and their level of responsibility. *Senior drafters* translate preliminary drawings and plans into design layouts—scale drawings of the object to be built. *Detailers* draw each part shown on the layout giving dimensions, materials, and other information. *Checkers* examine drawings and specifications for errors. Supervised by experienced drafters, *tracers* make minor corrections and trace drawings for reproduction on paper or plastic film. Beginners usually start as tracers or junior drafters and work their way up through checker and detailer positions.

Ninety percent of all drafters work in private industry. Engineering and architectural firms employ the most; other large employers are fabricated metals, electrical equipment, machinery, and construction firms. About 20,000 drafters work for federal, state, and local government agencies. The U.S. Department of Defense is the main federal employer; state and local governments employ drafters mainly in highway and public works departments.

Places of Employment and Working Conditions   Drafters work in all areas of the country with the largest concentrations in industrialized areas.

Working areas are usually pleasant, but drafters do very detailed work and must often sit for long periods of time.

Qualifications, Education, and Training   Drafters need good eyesight, manual dexterity, and drawing ability and must be able to do accurate, detailed work. They must have the ability to work as part of a team. In some specialized fields, artistic ability is also necessary.

High school courses should include mechanical drawing, science, computers, and mathematics. Shop skills are also helpful.

Drafting skills may be acquired in several ways. Vocational and technical high schools provide enough training for entry-level jobs at companies with on-the-job training programs. Technical institutes, junior and community colleges, and extension divisions of universities provide training for full-time and evening students. The armed forces also train drafters.

Due to the increasing use of computer-aided design systems, persons trained in electronic drafting will have the best prospects for employment.

Potential and Advancement   There are about 345,000 drafters and the field is expected to grow substantially. Job opportunities should be fairly good into the mid-1990s with the best job opportunities for those with an associate (two-year) degree or other formal training.

Experienced drafters can advance to senior drafter and supervisory positions. Some drafters become independent designers or continue their education to transfer to engineering positions.

Income   Median annual earnings of drafters who worked year round, full time were about $21,400 in 1986; the middle 50 percent earned between $16,500 and $29,000 annually. Ten percent earned less than $13,600 and 10 percent, more than $38,500.

In private industry, beginning drafters averaged about $13,054 a year in 1986, while more experienced drafters averaged between $15,854 and $24,652 a year. Senior drafters averaged about $31,004 a year.

Additional Sources of Information

American Institute for Design and Drafting
966 Hungerford Drive
Suite 10–13
Rockville, MD 20850

International Federation of Professional and Technical Engineers
8701 Georgia Ave., Suite 701
Silver Spring, MD 20910

Electrical/Electronics Engineer

The Job   Electrical and electronics engineering is the largest branch of engineering. These engineers design and develop electrical and electronic equipment and products. They may work in power generation and transmission; machinery controls; lighting and wiring for buildings, automobiles, and aircraft; computers; radar; communications equipment; missile guidance systems; or consumer goods such as television sets and appliances.

Engineers in this field usually specialize in a major area such as communications, computers, or power distribution equipment or in a subdivision such as aviation electronic systems. Many are involved in research, development, and design of new products; others in manufacturing and sales.

The main employers of electrical engineers are companies that manufacture electrical and electronic equipment, aircraft and parts, business machines, and professional and scientific equipment. Telephone, telegraph and electric light and power companies also employ many electrical engineers. Others work for construction firms, engineering consulting firms, and government agencies. A number of them work in the field of nuclear energy.

Places of Employment and Working Conditions

Engineers are employed in all areas of the country, in towns and cities of all sizes as well as rural areas, with some specialties concentrated in certain areas.

Qualifications, Education, and Training

The ability to think analytically, a capacity for detail, and the ability to work as part of a team are all necessary. Good communications skills are important.

Mathematics and the sciences must be emphasized in high school.

A bachelor's degree in engineering is the minimum requirement in this field. In a typical curriculum, the first two years are spent in the study of basic sciences such as physics and chemistry and mathematics, introductory engineering, and some liberal arts courses. The remaining years are usually devoted to specialized engineering courses. Engineering programs can last from four to six years. Those requiring five or six years to complete may award a master's degree or may provide a cooperative plan of study plus practical work experience with a nearby industry.

Because of rapid changes in technology, many engineers continue their education throughout their careers. A graduate degree is necessary for most teaching and research positions and for many management jobs. Some persons obtain graduate degrees in business administration.

Engineering graduates usually work under the supervision of an experienced engineer or in a company training program until they become acquainted with the requirements of a particular company or industry.

All states require licensing of engineers whose work may affect life, health, or property or who offer their services to the public. Those who are licensed, about one-third of all engineers, are called registered engineers. Requirements include graduation from an accredited engineering school, four years of experience, and a written examination.

Potential and Advancement

There are about 401,000 electrical engineers. Increased demand for computers, communications, and military electronics is expected to provide ample job opportunities for electrical engineers into the 1990s. A sharp rise or fall in government spending for defense could change this picture in either direction.

Income

Starting salaries for engineers with the bachelor's degree are significantly higher than starting salaries of college graduates in other fields. Ac-

the College Placement Council, engineering graduates with a degree and no experience averaged about $27,900 a year in private 1986; those with a master's degree and no experience, $33,100 a year; and those with a Ph.D., $42,200. Starting offers for those with the bachelor's degree vary by branch. Engineers in private industry in 1986 averaged $27,866 at the most junior level, and $79,021 at senior managerial levels. Experienced mid-level engineers with no supervisory responsibilities averaged $42,677.

Additional Sources of Information

Institute of Electrical and Electronics Engineers
United States Activities Board
345 E. 47th Street
New York, NY 10017

Engineers' Council for Professional Development
345 East 47th Street
New York, NY 10017

National Society of Professional Engineers
1420 King Street
Alexandria, VA 22314

American Society for Engineering Education
11 Dupont Circle
Suite 200
Washington, DC 20036

Society of Women Engineers
United Engineering Center
345 East 47th Street
New York, NY 10017

Engineer

The Job   Engineers apply the theories and principles of science and mathematics to practical technical problems. This is one of the largest professions in the country, second only to teaching.

Most engineers specialize in one of the 25 major branches of engineering. Within these branches there are over 85 subdivisions, and engineers may further specialize in one industry, such as motor vehicles, or one field of technology, such as propulsion or guidance systems. This job description provides an overall picture of engineering as a career. Information on major branches of this profession appear elsewhere in this book (Aerospace Engineer, Civil Engineer, and so forth).

In general, engineers in a particular field may be involved in research, design, and development; production and operation; maintenance; time and cost estimation; sales and technical assistance; or administration and management. Engineers usually work as part of a team and, regardless of specialty, may apply their knowledge across several fields. For example, an electrical engineer can work in the medical field, computers, missile guidance systems, or electric power distribution. An agricultural engineer may design farm equipment, manage water resources, or work in soil conservation.

While more than half of all engineers work for manufacturing industries, about 31 percent work in nonmanufacturing industries such as construction, public utilities, engineering and architectural services, and business and consulting services.

Federal, state, and local government agencies employ about 14 percent of all engineers. Federally employed engineers work mainly for the Departments of Defense, Interior, Agriculture, Transportation, and NASA. In state and local governments, engineers will usually work for highway and public works departments.

About 4 percent of all engineers teach and do research.

Women make up only 2 percent of the total in this profession. Many firms, however, as well as engineering schools, are actively recruiting women to comply with affirmative action programs and other government regulations on equal employment opportunity.

A related job is: industrial designer.

Places of Employment and Working Conditions

Engineers are employed in all areas of the country, in towns and cities of all sizes as well as rural areas, with some specialties concentrated in certain areas.

Most engineers work indoors but some, depending on specialty, work outdoors or at remote locations.

Qualifications, Education, and Training

The ability to think analytically, a capacity for detail, and the ability to work as part of a team are all necessary. Good communication skills are important.

Mathematics and the sciences must be emphasized in high school.

A bachelor's degree in engineering is the minimum requirement in this field. In a typical curriculum, the first two years are spent in the study of basic sciences such as physics and chemistry and mathematics, introductory engineering, and some liberal arts courses. The remaining years are usually devoted to specialized engineering courses. Engineering programs can last from four to six years. Those requiring five or six years to complete may award a master's degree or may provide a cooperative plan of study plus practical work experience with a nearby industry.

Because of rapid changes in technology, many engineers continue their education throughout their careers. A graduate degree is necessary for most teaching and research positions and for many management jobs. Some specialties such as nuclear engineering are taught only at the graduate level. Some persons obtain graduate degrees in business administration or in a field such as law (for patent attorneys).

Engineering graduates usually work under the supervision of an experienced engineer or in a company training program until they become acquainted with the requirements of a particular company or industry.

All states require licensing of engineers whose work may affect life, health, or property or who offer their services to the public. Those who are licensed, about one-third of all engineers, are called registered engineers. Requirements include graduation from an accredited engineering school, four years of experience, and a written examination.

Potential and Advancement
There are approximately 1.4 million engineers. The employment outlook for engineers is good for the foreseeable future with some specialties more in demand than others. In general, qualified engineers and available job openings will be in balance.

Experienced engineers may advance to administrative and management positions. Many of the highest-level executives in private industry started their careers as engineers.

Income
Starting salaries for engineers with the bachelor's degree are significantly higher than starting salaries of college graduates in other fields. According to the College Placement Council, engineering graduates with a bachelor's degree and no experience averaged about $27,900 a year in private industry in 1986; those with a master's degree and no experience, $33,100 a year; and those with a Ph.D., $42,200. Starting offers for those with the bachelor's degree vary by branch. Engineers in private industry in 1986 averaged $27,866 at the most junior level, and $79,021 at senior managerial levels. Experienced mid-level engineers with no supervisory responsibilities averaged $42,677.

Additional Sources of Information

Engineers' Council for Professional Development
345 East 47th Street
New York, NY 10017

National Society of Professional Engineers
1420 King Street
Alexandria, VA 22314

American Society for Engineering Education
11 Dupont Circle
Suite 200
Washington, DC 20036

Society of Women Engineers
United Engineering Center
345 East 47th Street
New York, NY 10017

Forester

The Job   The forest lands of the United States—whether publicly or privately owned—must be carefully and efficiently managed if they are to survive. It is the work of the professional forester to develop, manage, and protect forest lands and their resources of timber, water, wildlife, forage, and recreation areas. If properly protected and managed, these resources can be utilized repeatedly without being destroyed.

Foresters often specialize in one type of work such as timber management, outdoor recreation, or forest economics. In these capacities, they might plan and supervise the planting and cutting of trees or devote themselves to watershed management, wildlife protection, disease and insect control, fire prevention, or the development and supervision of recreation areas.

About two-fifths of all foresters work for private industries such as pulp and paper, lumber, logging, and milling companies. The federal government employs about one-fourth of all foresters, most of them in the Forest Service of the Department of Agriculture. Others do research, teach at the college and university level, or work as consultants. State and local governments also typically employ foresters.

Related jobs are: environmentalist, soil scientist, soil conservationist.

Places of Employment and Working Conditions

Foresters are employed in just about every state, but the largest number are employed in the heavily forested areas of the northwest, northeast, and southern states.

Foresters, especially beginners, spend a great deal of time outdoors in all kinds of weather and often at remote locations. During emergencies such as fires and rescue missions, they may work long hours under difficult and dangerous conditions.

Qualifications, Education, and Training

Anyone interested in forestry as a career should be physically hardy, enjoy working outdoors, and be willing to work in remote areas.

A bachelor's degree with a major in forestry is the minimum requirement, but employers prefer to hire applicants with advanced degrees. About 50 colleges offer degrees in forestry, most of them accredited by the Society of American Foresters. Scientific and technical forestry subjects, liberal arts, and communication skills are emphasized along with courses in forest economics and business administration. All schools encourage work experience in forestry or conservation, and many of the colleges require at least one summer at a college-operated field camp.

Potential and Advancement

About 23,000 persons are employed as foresters. Employment opportunities are expected to grow somewhat, but the number of degrees being awarded in forestry will soon exceed the number of job openings, creating competition among applicants. Those with advanced degrees or several years of experience have the best chance of securing a job. Job opportunities will probably be greatest with private owners of timberland and with state governmental agencies in cooperative federal-state programs of fire prevention, insect and disease control, and recreation.

Advancement in this field depends on experience with federally employed foresters able to advance through supervisory positions to regional forest supervisors or to top administrative positions. In private industry, experienced foresters may advance to top managerial positions within a company.

Income

Most graduates entering the federal government as foresters, range managers, or soil conservationists in 1987 with a bachelor's degree started at $14,800 a year. Those with a master's degree could start at $22,500. Holders of doctorates could start at $27,200 or, in research positions, at $32,600. In 1986, the average federal salary for foresters was $32,800; for range conservationists, $28,500; and for soil conservationists, $29,600.

Salaries in state and local government and in private industry were generally lower.

Additional Sources of Information

Society of American Foresters
5400 Grosvenor Lane
Bethesda, MD 20814

American Forest Council
1250 Connecticut Avenue, NW
Washington, DC 20036

U.S. Department of Agriculture
Forest Service
P.O. Box 2417
Washington, DC 20013

Forestry Technician

The Job   Forestry technicians assist foresters in the care and management of forest lands and their resources. They estimate timber production, inspect for insect damage, supervise surveying and road-building crews, work in flood control and water quality programs, supervise firefighting crews, supervise planting and reforestation programs, and maintain forest areas for hunting, camping, and other recreational uses.

About half of all forestry technicians work for private logging, lumber, paper, mining, and railroad companies. The federal government employs about an equal number. Many of the technicians employed by the federal and state governments work during summer only or during the spring and fall fire seasons.

There are few women in this field, but their number is increasing.

Places of Employment and Working Conditions

Forestry technicians work throughout the country in just about every state.

Outdoor work in all kinds of weather is the norm for this job field. In emergencies such as forest fires and floods, the working hours are very long and the work can be dangerous. In many areas, the work is seasonal.

Qualifications, Education, and Training

Good physical condition, stamina, love of the outdoors, and ability to work with or without supervision and to work with a variety of people are all necessary for a forestry technician.

High school should include as many science courses as possible.

Some technicians acquire their training through experience on firefighting crews, in recreation work, or in tree nurseries. Because this is a very competitive job field, however, those with specialized training in forestry have better opportunities for full-time employment.

One- and two-year courses for forestry technicians are available in technical institutes, junior colleges, and colleges and universities. Subjects studied include mathematics, biology and botany, land surveying, tree identification, aerial photography interpretation, and timber harvesting.

Potential and Advancement

There are about 11,000 full-time forestry technicians; an equal number are employed seasonally. This field is expected to grow steadily, but applicants will continue to exceed job openings due to the popularity of the work. Private industry will continue to provide the bulk of the full-time positions.

Income

Beginning salaries range from $12,000 to $15,000. Experienced forestry technicians earn $18,000 or $20,000 a year.

Additional Sources of Information

American Forestry Association
1516 P Street, NW
Washington, DC 20005

U.S. Department of Agriculture
Forest Service
P.O. Box 2417
Washington, DC 20013

Society of American Foresters
5400 Grosvenor Lane
Bethesda, MD 20814

Geographer

The Job   Geographers study and analyze the distribution of land forms; climate; soils; vegetation; and mineral, water, and human resources. These studies help to explain the patterns of human settlement.

Over half of all geographers are employed by colleges and universities. The federal government also employs many geographers for mapping, intelligence work, and remote sensing interpretation. State and local governments employ geographers on planning and development commissions.

Textbook and map publishers; travel agencies; manufacturing firms; real estate developers; and insurance, communications, and transportation companies employ geographers. Those with additional training in another discipline such as economics, sociology, or urban planning have a wider range of job opportunities and can work in many other fields.

Cartographers design and construct maps and charts. They also conduct research in surveying and mapping procedures. They work with aerial photographs and analyze data from remote sensing equipment on satellites.

About 15 percent of all geographers in the United States are women.

Places of Employment and Working Conditions   Geographers are employed throughout the country and on foreign assignment as well. The largest single concentration of geographers is in the Washington, D.C., area.

Field work sometimes entails assignment to remote areas and primitive regions of the world. A geographer should be prepared for the physical and social hardships such relocation may require.

Qualifications, Education, and Training   Anyone interested in this field should enjoy reading, studying, and research and be able to work independently. Good communication skills are also necessary.

High school should include as many mathematics and science courses as are possible.

A bachelor's degree with a major in geography is the first step for a would-be geographer. Course work should also include some specialty fields such as cartography, aerial photography, or statistical analysis.

Advanced degrees are required for most teaching positions and for advancement in business and government; a Ph.D. is necessary for the top jobs. Mathematics, statistics, and computer science are of increasing importance in graduate studies; students interested in foreign regional geography are usually required to take a foreign language as well.

Potential and Advancement
There are about 15,000 people working as geographers. In general, the field will grow, but some areas will offer more job opportunities than others. College and university teaching positions will remain about the same, and job openings will occur only to replace those who retire, die, or leave the field. The federal government will employ a growing number of geographers and cartographers as will state and local governments. Private industry will provide the largest increase in job openings in this field. Persons with only a bachelor's degree will face competition for jobs.

Advancement in this field depends on experience and additional education.

Income
Median annual earnings of all social scientists were about $29,600 in 1986. The middle 50 percent earned between $21,800 and $39,800 annually. The lowest 10 percent earned under $15,000, while the highest 10 percent earned over $51,000.

According to the College Placement Council, persons with a bachelor's degree in a social science field received starting offers averaging about $21,100 a year in 1986.

According to a 1985 National Science Foundation survey, the median annual salary of doctoral social scientists ranged from $37,200 to $46,100.

Additional Sources of Information

Association of American Geographers
1710 16th Street, NW
Washington, DC 20009

Geologist

The Job   By examining surface rocks and rock samples drilled from beneath the surface, geologists study the structure, composition, and history of the earth's crust. Their work is important in the search for mineral resources and oil and in the study of predicting earthquakes. Geologists are also employed to advise on the construction of buildings, dams, and highways.

Geologists study plant and animal fossils as well as minerals and rocks. Some specialize in the study of the ocean floor or the composition of other plants. *Vulcanologists* study active and inactive volcanoes and lava flows. *Mineralogists* analyze and classify minerals and precious stones.

Over half of all geologists work in private industry mainly for petroleum and mining companies. The federal government employs over 2,000 geologists in the U.S. Geological Survey, the Bureau of Mines, and the Bureau of Reclamation. State and local governments employ geologists in highway construction and survey work.

Colleges and universities, nonprofit research institutions, and museums also employ geologists.

Only about 4 percent of all geologists are women. Traditionally, this has been a male field, but women with a strong background in mathematics and science are entering the field and liking it.

Related jobs are: geophysicist, meteorologist, and oceanographer.

Places of Employment and Working Conditions   Five
states account for most jobs in geology: Texas, California, Louisiana, Colorado, and Oklahoma. Other areas with large oil and mineral deposits also provide job opportunities. American companies often send their geologists to overseas locations for varying periods of time.

Much of the work done by geologists is out-of-doors, often at remote locations. Geologists also cover many miles on foot. Those involved in mining often work underground; geologists in petroleum research often work on offshore oil rigs.

Qualifications, Education, and Training   Curiosity, analytical
thinking, and physical stamina are all necessary for a geologist.

High school work should include as much science and mathematics as are possible.

A bachelor's degree in geology or a related field is the basic preparation and is adequate for some entry-level jobs. Teaching and research positions require advanced degrees with specialization in one particular branch of geology.

Potential and Advancement   About 34,000 people work as geologists. This is a growing field, and job opportunities will increase steadily as the nation pushes for development of petroleum and other resources.

Those with advanced degrees will have the most job opportunities and the best chances for promotion.

Income   Surveys by the College Placement Council indicate that graduates with bachelor's degrees in physical and earth sciences received an average starting offer of $19,200 a year in 1986.

In the federal government in early 1987, geologists and geophysicists having a bachelor's degree could begin at $14,822 or $18,358 a year, depending on their college records. Those having a master's degree could start at $18,358 or $22,458 a year; those having the Ph.D. degree, at $27,172 or $32,567. In 1986, the average salary for geologists in the federal government was about $37,500 a year and for geophysicists, about $40,900 a year.

Additional Sources of Information

American Geological Institute
4220 King Street
Alexandria, VA 22302

Interagency Board of U.S. Civil Service Examiners for Washington, DC
1900 E Street, NW
Washington, DC 20415

Geophysicist

The Job   In general terms, geophysicists study the earth—its composition and physical aspects and its electric, magnetic, and gravitational fields. They usually specialize in one of three general phases of the science—solid earth, fluid earth, or upper atmosphere—and some also study other planets.

Solid earth geophysicists search for oil and mineral deposits, map the earth's surface, and study earthquakes. This field includes *exploration geophysicists,* who use seismic prospecting techniques (sound waves) to locate oil and mineral deposits; *seismologists,* who study the earth's interior and earth vibrations caused by earthquakes and man-made explosions, explore for oil and minerals, and provide information for use in constructing bridges, dams, and large buildings (by determining where bedrock is located in relation to the surface); and *geologists* who study the size, shape, and gravitational field of the earth and other planets and whose principal task is the precise measurement of the earth's surface.

Hydrologists are concerned with the fluid earth. They study the distribution, circulation, and physical properties of underground and surface waters including glaciers, snow, and permafrost. Those who are concerned with water supplies, irrigation, flood control, and soil erosion study rainfall and its rate of infiltration into the soil. *Oceanographers* are also sometimes classified as geophysical scientists.

Geophysicists who study the earth's atmosphere and electric and magnetic fields and compare them with other planets include: *geomagneticians,* who study the earth's magnetic field; *paleomagneticians,* who study rocks and lava flows to learn about past magnetic fields; and *planetologists,* who study the composition and atmosphere of the moon, planets, and other bodies in the solar system. They gather data from geophysical instruments placed on interplanetary space probes or from equipment used by astronauts during the Apollo missions. *Meteorologists* sometimes are also classified as geophysical scientists.

Most geophysicists work in private industry chiefly for petroleum and natural gas companies. Others are in mining, exploration, and consulting firms or in research institutes. A few are independent consultants doing geophysical prospecting on a fee or contract basis.

Approximately 2,300 geophysicists work for the federal government mainly in the U.S. Geological Survey, the National Oceanic and Atmospheric Administration, and the Department of Defense. Other employers are colleges and universities, state governments, and research institutions. Some geophysicists are also employed by American firms overseas.

New geophysicists usually begin their careers doing field mapping or exploration. Some assist senior geophysicists in research work.

Places of Employment and Working Conditions   In the United States, many geophysicists are employed in southwestern and western states and along the Gulf Coast where large oil and natural gas fields are typically located.

Many geophysicists work outdoors and must be willing to travel for extended periods. Some work at research stations in remote areas or aboard ships and aircraft. When not in the field, geophysicists work in modern well-equipped laboratories and offices.

Qualifications, Education, and Training   Geophysicists should be curious, analytical, and able to communicate effectively and should like to work as part of a team.

High school courses should include as many science courses as possible and mathematics.

A bachelor's degree in geophysics or in a geophysical specialty is acceptable for most beginning jobs. A bachelor's degree in a related field of science or engineering is also adequate, provided courses in geophysics, physics, geology, mathematics, chemistry, and engineering have been included.

About 75 colleges and universities award a bachelor's degree in geophysics. Other training programs offered include geophysical technology, geophysical engineering, engineering geology, petroleum geology, and geodesy.

More than 60 universities grant master's and Ph.D. degrees in geophysics. Geophysicists doing research or supervising exploration should have graduate training in geophysics or a related science, and those planning to do basic research or teach college level need a Ph.D. degree.

Potential and Advancement   About 12,000 people work as geophysicists; employment opportunities are expected to grow slowly through the 1990s. The number of qualified geophysicists, however, fall short of requirements despite slow growth. As known deposits of petroleum and other minerals are depleted, petroleum and mining companies will need increasing numbers of geophysicists to find less accessible fuel and mineral deposits. In addition, geophysicists with advanced training will be needed to research alternate energy sources such as geothermal power (use of steam from the earth's interior) and to study solar and cosmic radiation and radioactivity. Federal agencies are also expected to hire more geophysicists for research and development in the earth sciences, energy research, and environmental protection.

Geophysicists with experience can advance to jobs such as project leader or program manager. Some achieve management positions or go into research.

Income   Surveys by the College Placement Council indicate that graduates with bachelor's degrees in physical and earth sciences received an average starting offer of $19,200 a year in 1986.

In the federal government in early 1987, geologists and geophysicists having a bachelor's degree could begin at $14,822 or $18,358 a year, depending on their college records. Those having a master's degree could start at $18,358 or $22,458 a year; those having the Ph.D. degree, at $27,172 or $32,567. In 1986, the average salary for geologists in the federal government was about $37,500 a year and for geophysicists, about $40,900 a year.

Additional Sources of Information

American Geophysical Union
2000 Florida Avenue, NW
Washington, DC 20009

Society of Exploration Geophysicists
P.O. Box 70240
Tulsa, OK 74170

Industrial Designer

The Job   Industrial designers develop new styles and designs for products ranging from pencil sharpeners and dishwashers to automobiles. Some specialize in package design or the creation of trademarks; others plan the entire layout of commercial buildings such as supermarkets.

Industrial designers combine artistic talent with knowledge of materials and production methods. Teamwork is necessary in this field, and input from many people goes into a finished product. Working closely with engineers, production personnel, and sales and marketing experts, industrial designers thoroughly research a product. They prepare detailed drawings, then a scale model of a new design. After approval of a design, a full-scale working model is built and tested before production begins.

Most industrial designers work for large manufacturing firms where they fill day-to-day design needs and work on long-range planning of new products; or for design consulting firms that service a number of industrial companies. Some do freelance work or work for architectural and interior design firms. A few teach in colleges and universities or art schools.

There are very few women in this field.

Places of Employment and Working Conditions
Industrial designers work for manufacturing firms in all parts of the United States. Industrial design consultants work mainly in New York City, Chicago, Los Angeles, and San Francisco.

A five-day, 35- to 40-hour week is usual with occasional overtime necessary to meet deadlines.

Qualifications, Education, and Training
Creativity, artistic talent and drawing skills, the ability to see familiar objects in new ways, and communication skills are necessary. An industrial designer must be able to design to meet the needs and tastes of the public, not just to suit the designer's artistic ideas.

High school should include courses in art, mechanical drawing, and also mathematics.

Courses in industrial design are offered by art schools, technical schools, and colleges and universities. Most large manufacturing firms require a bachelor's degree in industrial design.

Thirty-three colleges and art schools offer programs that are either accredited by the National Association of Schools of Art or recognized by the Industrial Designers Society of America. These programs take four or five years and lead to a bachelor's degree in industrial design or fine arts. Some schools also offer a master's degree in industrial design.

Some schools require the submission of samples of artistic ability before acceptance into their industrial design programs. After graduation, job applicants are expected to show a portfolio of their work to demonstrate their creativity and design ability.

Potential and Advancement
There are about 35,000 industrial designers. This is a relatively small field with only limited growth expected in the foreseeable future. Job opportunities will be best for college graduates with degrees in industrial design.

Industrial designers may be promoted to supervisory positions with major responsibility for design of a specific product or group of products. Those with an established reputation sometimes start their own consulting firms.

Income
Median annual earnings of experienced full-time designers were almost $25,500 in 1986. The middle 50 percent earned between $16,800 and $34,400 a year. The bottom 10 percent earned less than $15,200, and the top 10 percent earned more than $46,500.

Earnings of self-employed designers vary greatly, depending on their talent and business ability, but generally are higher than those of salaried designers.

Additional Sources of Information

Industrial Designers Society of America
1142-E Walker Road
Great Falls, VA 22066

Industrial Engineer

The Job   Industrial engineers are concerned with people and methods while other engineers may usually be concerned with a product or progress. Industrial engineers determine the most efficient and effective way for a company to use the basic components of production—people, machines, and materials.

Industrial engineers develop management control systems for financial planning and cost analysis, design production planning and control systems, design time study and quality control programs, and survey possible plant locations for the best combination of raw materials, transportation, labor supply, and taxes.

About two-thirds of all industrial engineers are employed by manufacturing industries, but, because their skills can be used in almost any type of company, industrial engineers work in many industries that don't employ other types of engineers. They may work for insurance companies, banks, hospitals, retail organizations, and other large business firms, as well as more traditional engineering employers such as construction companies, mining firms, and utility companies.

Related jobs include: office manager, interior designer/decorator, systems analyst.

Places of Employment and Working Conditions   Industrial engineers work in all parts of the country and are concentrated in industrialized and commercial areas.

This is a physically active engineering specialty involving daily visits to departments within the plants, offices, and grounds of the employer as well as travel to possible plant locations.

Qualifications, Education, and Training
The ability to think analytically, a capacity for detail, and the ability to work as part of a team are all necessary. Good communication skills are important.

Mathematics and the sciences must be emphasized in high school.

A bachelor's degree in engineering is the maximum requirement in this field. In a typical curriculum, the first two years are spent in the study of basic sciences such as physics and chemistry and mathematics, introductory engineering, and some liberal arts courses. The remaining years are usually devoted to specialized engineering courses. Engineering programs can last from four to six years. Those that require five or six years to complete may award a master's degree or may provide a cooperative plan of study plus practical work experience with a nearby industry.

Because of rapid changes in technology, many engineers continue their education throughout their careers. A graduate degree is necessary for most teaching and research positions and for many management jobs. Some persons obtain graduate degrees in business administration.

Engineering graduates usually work under the supervision of an experienced engineer or in a company training program until they become acquainted with the requirements of a particular company or industry.

All states require licensing of engineers whose work may affect life, health, or property or who offer their services to the public. Those who are licensed, about one-third of all engineers, are called registered engineers. Requirements include graduation from an accredited engineering school, four years of experience, and a written examination.

Potential and Advancement
There are about 117,000 industrial engineers. Job opportunities in this field are expected to increase substantially in the 1990s because of the increased complexity and expanding use of automated processes and increased recognition of the importance of scientific management and safety engineering in reducing costs and increasing productivity.

Income
Starting salaries for engineers with the bachelor's degree are significantly higher than starting salaries of college graduates in other fields. According to the College Placement Council, engineering graduates with a bachelor's degree and no experience averaged about $27,900 a year in private industry in 1986; those with a master's degree and no experience, $33,100 a year; and those with a Ph.D., $42,200. Starting offers for those with the bachelor's degree vary by branch. Engineers in private industry in 1986 averaged $27,866 at the most junior level, and $79,021 at senior managerial levels. Experienced mid-level engineers with no supervisory responsibilities averaged $42,677.

Additional Sources of Information

Institute of Industrial Engineers
25 Technology Park/Atlanta
Norcross, GA 30092

Engineers' Council for Professional Development
345 East 47th Street
New York, NY 10017

National Society of Professional Engineers
1420 King Street
Alexandria, VA 22314

American Society for Engineering Education
11 Dupont Circle
Suite 200
Washington, DC 20036

Society of Women Engineers
United Engineering Center
345 East 47th Street
New York, NY 10017

Landscape Architect

The Job   Landscape architects design the outdoor areas of commercial buildings and private homes, public parks and playgrounds, real estate developments, airports, shopping centers, hotels and resorts, and public housing. Their work not only beautifies these areas but helps them to function efficiently as well.

A landscape architect prepares detailed maps and plans showing all existing and planned features and, once the plans are approved, may accept bids from landscape contractors on the work to be done. In addition to planning the placement of trees, shrubs, and walkways, the landscape architect supervises any necessary grading, construction, and planting.

Most landscape architects are self-employed or work for architectural, landscape architectural, or engineering firms. State and local government agencies employ landscape architects for forest management; water storage; public housing, city planning, and urban renewal projects; highways, parks, and recreation areas. The federal government employs them in the Departments of Agriculture, Defense, and Interior. A few are employed by landscape contractors.

Beginners in this field are given simple drafting assignments, working their way up by preparing specifications and construction details and other aspects of project design. It is usually two or three years before they are allowed to handle a design through all stages of development.

Less than 5 percent of all landscape architects are women. Since this field requires a flair for art and design, talents that many women possess, it could prove to be a good job opportunity field for women who like to work out-of-doors.

Related jobs are: environmentalist, farmer, floral designer, forester, forestry technician, urban planner.

Places of Employment and Working Conditions Landscape architects work throughout the United States, but most job opportunities exist in the large metropolitan areas of the East and West. The biggest growth in this job field in recent years is in the Southwest.

Salaried employees in this field usually work a 40-hour week; self-employed landscape architects often work much longer hours. Although a great many of an architect's hours are spent outdoors, a substantial number of hours are also spent indoors in planning and mapping activities.

Qualifications, Education, and Training Creative ability, appreciation of nature, talent in art and design, and the ability to work in detail are important. Business ability is necessary for those who intend to open their own landscape architectural firms.

High school should include courses in biology, botany, art, mathematics, and mechanical drawing. Summer jobs for landscaping contractors or plant nurseries provide good experience.

About 40 colleges offer bachelor's degree programs in landscape architecture that are approved by the American Society of Landscape Architects. Sixty other schools offer programs or courses in this field. Bachelor-degree programs take four or five years to complete.

A license is required in most states for the independent practice of landscape architecture. Requirements include a degree from an accredited school of landscape architecture, two to four years of experience, and a passing grade on a uniform national licensing examination. In some states, six to eight years of apprenticeship training under an experienced landscape architect may sometimes be substituted for college training.

Potential and Advancement There are about 18,000 practicing professional landscape architects. The outlook is for rapid growth in this field through the 1990s, although any periods of downturn in the construction industry could cause temporary slow periods. City and regional planning programs, interest in environmental protection, and the growth of transportation systems and recreational areas will contribute to the demand for qualified landscape architects as will the general growth in population.

Landscape architects usually advance by moving to a larger firm, by becoming associates in their firm, or by opening their own businesses.

Income According to limited data, graduates with a bachelor's degree in landscape architecture usually started at about $18,000 in 1986; those with a master's degree at about $22,000. Although salaries for experienced landscape architects varied by location and experience, they generally earned between $25,000 and $50,000 per year. In addition, those who are partners in well-established firms may earn much more than their salaried employees, but their incomes may fluctuate with changing business conditions.

Additional Sources of Information

American Society of Landscape Architects
1733 Connecticut Avenue, NW
Washington, DC 20009

U.S. Department of Agriculture
Forest Service
Washington, DC 20250

Life Scientist

The Job From the smallest living cell to the largest animals and plants, life scientists study living organisms and their life processes. Life scientists usually work in one of three broad areas: agriculture, biology, or medicine.

About one-third of all life scientists are involved in research and development—doing basic research or applying it in medicine, increasing agricultural yields, and improving the environment. Another one-third hold management and administrative positions in zoos and botanical gardens and in programs dealing with the testing of foods and drugs. Some work in technical sales and service jobs for industrial firms, or they may work as consultants to business and government.

Some life scientists call themselves *biologists,* but the usual method of classification is according to the type of organism studied or the specific activity performed. *Botanists* deal with plants—studying, classifying, and developing cures for plant disease. *Agronomists* work with food crops to increase yields, to control disease, pests, and weeds, and to prevent soil erosion. *Horticulturists* are concerned with orchard and garden plants such as fruit and nut trees, vegetables, and flowers.

Zoologists, who study animal life, have titles that reflect the group they study: *ornithologists* study birds, *entomologists* study insects, and *mammalogists* study mammals. *Animal husbandry specialists* are involved in breeding, feeding, and controlling disease in domestic animals. *Embryologists* study the development of animals from fertilized egg through the birth or hatching process.

Microbiologists investigate the growth and characteristics of microscopic organisms such as bacteria, viruses, and molds. *Medical microbiologists* study the relationship between bacteria and disease and the various effects of antibiotics on bacteria.

Pathologists study the effect of diseases, parasites, insects, or drugs on human cells and tissue. *Pharmacologists* test the effect of drugs, gases, poisons, and other substances on animals and use the results of their research to develop new or improved drugs and medicines.

Anatomists, ecologists, geneticists, and *nutritionists* are also life scientists. About one-half of these life scientists are employed in colleges and universities usually in medical schools and state agricultural colleges. About one-fourth of these professionals are employed by the federal government, almost all of them in the Department of Agriculture. The remainder are employed by private industry in drug, food products, and agricultural-related industries.

About 20 percent of all life scientists are women, and approximately 40 percent of the Ph.D. degrees awarded in this field go to women.

Related jobs are: biochemist, environmentalist, oceanographer, soil scientist, and veterinarian.

Places of Employment and Working Conditions   Life scientists work throughout the United States with the largest concentrations in metropolitan areas.

Most life scientists work in laboratories; some jobs, however, require outdoor work and strenuous physical labor. Working hours may be irregular in some specialties due to the nature of the research or activity under way.

Qualifications, Education, and Training

The ability to work independently and to function as part of a team is necessary for a career in the life sciences. Good communication skills are also necessary. Physical stamina is necessary in some of the specialty areas that require outdoor work.

High school courses should include as much science and mathematics courses as possible.

Almost all liberal arts programs include a biology major, and life science students should also include chemistry and physics courses. Some colleges offer bachelor's degrees in specific life sciences; many state universities offer programs in agricultural specialties. A bachelor's degree is adequate preparation for testing and inspection jobs and for advanced technician jobs in the medical field. With courses in education, it is also adequate background for high school teaching positions.

An advanced degree is required for most jobs in the life sciences. A master's degree is sufficient for some jobs in applied research and college teaching, but a Ph.D. is required for most teaching positions at the college level, for independent research, and for many administration jobs. A health-science degree is necessary for some jobs in the medical field.

Requirements for advanced degrees usually include fieldwork and laboratory research.

Potential and Advancement

There are approximately 205,000 life scientists in the United States including 40,000 engaged in agricultural sciences and about 65,000 in medical fields. Job opportunities in the life sciences will increase, but some fields will be better than others: Medical and environmental research will grow, while teaching opportunities will not. Life-science degrees can also be useful in other fields, however, such as health care and laboratory technology.

Advancement in this field depends on experience and is usually limited to those with advanced degrees.

Income

Life scientists earn relatively high salaries with earnings of all life scientists averaging above $35,000 a year.

In private industry, beginners with a bachelor's degree average $25,000 a year. Pharmacologists are the highest paid in private industry.

Life scientists who have an M.D. degree earn more than other life scientists but not as much as physicians in private practice.

The federal government starts beginners with a bachelor's degree at $16,700 to $23,000 depending on their academic record. Starting salaries for life scientists with a master's degree are about $25,000 or $40,000, depending on academic record or experience; those with a Ph.D. degree start at about $35,000 or $60,000.

Additional Sources of Information

American Institute of Biological Sciences
730 11th Street, NW
Washington, DC 20001

American Society for Horticultural Science
701 North Saint Asaph Street
Alexandria, VA 22314

American Physiological Society
Education Office
9650 Rockville Pike
Bethesda, MD 20014

U.S. Civil Service Commission
Washington Area Office
1900 E Street, NW
Washington, DC 20415

Mathematician

The Job   The work of mathematicians falls into two sometimes overlapping categories—applied and theoretical mathematics.

Theoretical or pure mathematicians develop new principles and seek new relationships between existing principles of mathematics. This basic knowledge is the foundation for much of the work in the second category, applied mathematics. In this area, mathematical theories are used to develop theories and techniques for solving practical problems in business, government, and the natural and social sciences. Mathematicians may work in statistics, actuarial jobs, computer programming, economics, or systems analysis.

Three-fourths of all mathematicians, usually theoretical mathematicians, work in colleges where they teach or do research. Mathematicians are found in the private sector in the aerospace, communications, machinery, and electrical equipment industries. The Department of Defense and National Aeronautics and Space Administration employ most of those who work for the federal government.

Related jobs are: economist, marketing research, statistician.

Places of Employment and Working Conditions
More than half of the mathematicians in this country are found in California, Illinois, Maryland, Massachusetts, New Jersey, and Pennsylvania. One-fourth live in New York City, Washington, D.C., and Los Angeles/Long Beach, California—primarily because these are large industrial areas and have many colleges and universities.

Qualifications, Education, and Training
Mathematicians need good reasoning ability and persistence in solving problems. In applied mathematics especially, they should be able to communicate effectively with nonmathematicians in the discussion and solution of practical problems.

A prospective mathematician should take as many mathematics courses as possible while still in high school and should obtain a bachelor's degree that includes courses in analytical geometry, calculus, differential equations, probability and statistics, mathematics analysis, and modern algebra.

Most positions in research or in university teaching require an advanced degree, frequently a Ph.D. Private industry and the government also prefer those with advanced degrees.

For work in applied mathematics, a background in a specialty field such as engineering, economics, or statistics is also necessary. This can be accomplished by including a minor in one of these fields while in college. In modern industry, knowledge of computer programming also is essential since most complex problems are now solved with the aid of computers.

Over 470 colleges and universities offer a master's degree program in mathematics and about 200 also offer a Ph.D. program. Candidates for graduate degrees in mathematics concentrate on a specific field such as algebra, geometry, or mathematical analyses and conduct research in addition to taking advanced courses.

Potential and Advancement
There are more than 45,000 mathematicians in the United States, with an estimated 15 percent of these being women. Employment opportunities for the coming decade are expected to be

few with competition keen for the available jobs. Fewest opportunities will exist in theoretical areas.

Applied mathematicians will need to possess a strong mathematical background as well as practical knowledge in a specialty field to qualify for jobs in industry and government. They will be hired to work in operations research, computer systems programming, and market research. New graduates may also find employment as secondary school teachers, if they meet teaching certification requirements.

Some states are meeting a shortage of teachers by permitting degreed mathematicians to work while fulfilling certification requirements over a three- to five-year period.

Many mathematicians advance by taking a lesser job, such as a research or teaching assistant, and continue their studies until they have attained the degree(s) necessary for the positions they really want.

Income   According to a 1986 College Placement Council survey, starting salary offers for mathematics graduates with a bachelor's degree averaged about $24,400 a year; for those with a master's degree, $30,600; and for new graduates having the Ph.D., $39,500. Starting salaries were generally higher in industry than in government or educational institutions.

According to a 1985 survey by the National Science Foundation, the median annual salary of mathematicians with a doctoral degree was $41,800; in business and industry, $51,200; in educational institutions, $40,200; and in the federal government, $48,300.

Additional Sources of Information

American Mathematical Society
P.O. Box 6248
Providence, RI 02940

Mathematical Association of America
1529 18th Street, NW
Washington, DC 20036

Society for Industrial and Applied Mathematics
117 South 17th Street
Philadelphia, PA 19103

Interagency Board of U.S. Civil Service Examiners
1900 E Street, NW
Washington, DC 20415

Mechanical Engineer

The Job   The production, transmission, and use of power is the concern of mechanical engineers. They design and develop power-producing machines such as internal combustion engines and rocket engines and power-using machines such as refrigeration systems, printing presses, and steel rolling mills.

The specific work of mechanical engineers varies greatly from industry to industry because of the wide application possibilities of their skills and training; many specialties within the field have developed as a result. These include motor vehicles, energy conversion systems, heating, and machines for specialized industries, to name a few. Many mechanical engineers are involved in research and testing while others work mainly in production and maintenance. Some utilize their training as a background for technical sales.

About three-fifths of all mechanical engineers are employed in manufacturing, mainly in the electrical equipment, transportation equipment, primary and fabricated metals, and machinery industries. Others work for engineering consulting firms, government agencies, and educational institutions. Mechanical engineers are the single largest group of engineers in the nuclear energy field.

Places of Employment and Working Conditions   Mechanical engineers work in all parts of the country with the heaviest concentrations in industrialized areas.

Qualifications, Education, and Training   The ability to think analytically, a capacity for detail, and the ability to work as part of a team are all necessary. Good communication skills are important.

Mathematics and the sciences must be emphasized in high school.

A bachelor's degree in engineering is the minimum requirement in this field. In a typical curriculum, the first two years are spent in the study of basic sciences such as physics and chemistry and mathematics, introductory engineering, and some liberal arts courses. The remaining years are usually devoted to specialized engineering courses. Engineering programs can last from four to six years. Those that require five or six years to complete may award a master's degree or may provide a cooperative plan of study plus practical work experience in a nearby industry.

Because of rapid changes in technology, many engineers continue their education throughout their careers. A graduate degree is necessary for most teaching and research positions and for many managerial jobs. Some specialties such as nuclear engineering are taught only at the graduate level. Some persons obtain graduate degrees in business administration.

Engineering graduates usually work under the supervision of an experienced engineer or in a company training program until they become acquainted with the requirements of a particular company or industry.

All states require licensing of engineers whose work may affect life, health, or property or who offer their services to the public. Those who are licensed, about one-third of all engineers, are called registered engineers. Requirements include graduation from an accredited engineering school, four years of experience, and a written examination.

Potential and Advancement   There are about 240,000 mechanical engineers. An increase in the demand for mechanical engineers—as a result of growth in the industrial machinery and machine tools field and the push to develop alternate energy sources—means ample job opportunities in this field into the 1990s.

Income   Starting salaries for engineers with the bachelor's degree are significantly higher than starting salaries of college graduates in other fields. According to the College Placement Council, engineering graduates with a bachelor's degree and no experience averaged about $27,900 a year in private industry in 1986; those with a master's degree and no experience, $33,100 a year; and those with a Ph.D., $42,200. Starting offers for those with the bachelor's degree vary by branch. Engineers in private industry in 1986 averaged $27,866 at the most junior level, and $79,021 at senior managerial levels. Experienced mid-level engineers with no supervisory responsibilities averaged $42,677.

Additional Sources of Information

The American Society of Mechanical Engineers
345 East 47th Street
New York, NY 10017

Engineers' Council for Professional Development
345 East 47th Street
New York, NY 10017

National Society of Professional Engineers
1420 King Street
Alexandria, VA 22314

American Society for Engineering Education
11 Dupont Circle
Suite 200
Washington, DC 20036

Society of Women Engineers
United Engineering Center
345 East 47th Street
New York, NY 10017

Medical Laboratory Technologist

The Job   Medical laboratory work often appeals to people who would like to work in the medical field but who are not necessarily interested in direct care of patients. Those who work in medical laboratories are involved in the analysis of blood, tissue samples, and body fluids. They use precision instruments, equipment, chemicals, and other materials to detect and diagnose diseases. In some instances, such as blood tests, they also gather the specimens to be analyzed.

The work of medical laboratory technologists is done under the direction of a pathologist (a physician who specializes in the causes and nature of disease) or other physician or scientist who specializes in clinical chemistry, microbiology, or other biological sciences.

Medical technologists, who have four years of training, usually perform a wide variety of tests in small laboratories; those in large laboratories usually specialize in a single area such as parisitology, blood banking, or hematology (study of blood cells). Some do research, develop laboratory techniques, or perform supervisory and administrative duties.

Medical laboratory technicians, who have two years of training, have much the same testing duties but do not have the in-depth knowledge of the technologists. Technicians may also specialize in a particular field but are not usually involved in administrative work.

Medical laboratory assistants have about one year of formal training. They assist the technologist and technicians in some routine tests and are generally responsible for the care and sterilization of laboratory equipment, including glassware and instruments, and do some recordkeeping.

Most technologists, technicians, and laboratory assistants work in hospital laboratories. Others work in physicians' offices, independent laboratories, blood banks, public health agencies and clinics, pharmaceutical firms, and research institutions. The federal government employs them in the U.S. Public Health Service, the armed forces, and Veterans Administration.

This is an excellent field for women who now hold a majority of the jobs in this field at all levels.

Places of Employment and Working Conditions
Work in this field is available in all areas of the country with the largest concentrations in the larger cities.

Medical laboratory personnel work a 40-hour week with night and weekend shifts if they are employed in a hospital. Laboratories are usually clean and well lighted and contain a variety of testing equipment and materials. Although unpleasant odors are sometimes present and the work involves the processing of specimens of many kinds of diseased tissue, few hazards exist because of careful attention to safety and sterilization procedures.

Qualifications, Education, and Training
A strong interest in science and the medical field is essential. Manual dexterity, good eyesight, and normal color vision are necessary along with attention to detail and accuracy and the ability to work under pressure and to take responsibility for one's own work.

High school students interested in this field should take courses in science and mathematics and should select a training program carefully.

Medical technologists must have a college degree and complete a specialized program in medical technology. This specialized training is offered by about 700 hospitals and schools in programs accredited by the American Medical Association (AMA). The programs are usually affiliated with a college or university. Some training programs require a bachelor's degree for entry; others require only three years of college and award a bachelor's degree at the completion of the training program. Those who wish to specialize must complete an additional 12 months of study with extensive lab work.

Advanced degrees in this field are offered by many universities and are a plus for anyone interested in teaching, research, or administration.

Technicians may receive training in two-year educational programs in junior colleges, in two-year courses at four-year colleges and universities, or in the armed forces. Some vocational and technical schools offer training programs for medical laboratory technicians, but not all are accredited by the AMA or the Accrediting Bureau of Medical Laboratory Schools.

Medical laboratory assistants usually receive on-the-job training. Some hospitals—and junior colleges and vocational schools in conjunction with a hospital—also conduct one-year training programs, some of which are accredited by the AMA. A high school diploma or equivalency diploma is necessary.

Medical technologists may be certified as medical technologist (MT-ASCP) by the Board of Registry of the American Society of Clinical Pathologists; medical technologist (MT) by the American Medical Technologists; or registered medical technologist (RMT) by the International Society of Clinical Laboratory Technology. These same organizations also certify technicians. Medical laboratory assistants are certified by the American Society of Clinical Pathologists.

A few states require technologists and technicians to be licensed. This usually takes the form of a written examination. Other states often require registration.

Potential and Advancement
There are about 240,000 persons employed as medical laboratory workers. Of these, approximately 40,000 are medical technologists. Medical laboratory technology is a good job opportunity field since, like the entire medical field, it is expected to grow steadily due to population growth and the increase in prepaid medical insurance programs. Job opportunities will probably be slightly better for technicians and assistants, because the increasing use of automated lab equipment will allow them to perform tests that previously required technologists. Technologists will be needed for supervisory and administrative positions, however, and will continue to be in demand in laboratories where their level of training is required by state regulations or employer preference.

Advancement depends on education and experience. Assistants can advance to the position of technician or technologist by completing the required education; technicians can advance to supervisory positions or complete the required education for technologists. Advancement to administrative positions is usually limited to technologists.

Income
Salaries of clinical laboratory personnel vary depending on the employer and geographic location. In general, those in large cities receive the highest salaries.

Starting salaries for medical technologists employed by hospitals, medical schools, and medical centers averaged about $19,600 a year in 1986, according to a survey conducted by the University of Texas Medical Branch. Beginning salaries for cytotechnologists averaged about $18,500; for histology technicians, about $15,600; and for medical laboratory technicians, about $14,700. According to the same survey, experienced medical technologists working in hospitals, medical schools, and medical centers averaged about $26,100 a year in 1986; cytotechnologists, about $23,800; histology technicians, about $20,000; and medical laboratory technicians, about $19,500.

Additional Sources of Information

American Society of Clinical Pathologists
Board of Registry
2100 W. Harrison Street
P.O. Box 12270
Chicago, IL 60612

American Society for Medical Technology
2021 L Street, NW
Washington, DC 20036

American Medical Technologists
710 Higgins Road
Park Ridge, IL 60068

Accrediting Bureau of Health Education Schools
Oak Manor Office
29089 U.S. 20 West
Elkhart, IN 46514

International Society for Clinical Laboratory Technology
818 Olive Street
St. Louis, MO 63101

Metallurgical Engineer

The Job   Metallurgical engineers develop methods to process and convert metals into usable forms. Other scientists who work in this field are called *metallurgists* or *materials scientists,* but the distinction between scientist and engineer in this field is so small as to be almost nonexistent.

There are three main branches of metallurgy—extractive or chemical, physical, and mechanical. *Extractive metallurgists* are engaged in the processes for extracting metals from ore, refining, and alloying. *Physical metallurgists* work with the nature, structure, and physical properties of metals and alloys to develop methods for converting them into final products. *Mechanical metalurgists* develop methods to work and shape metals. These include casting, forging, rolling, and drawing.

Over half of all metallurgical engineers are employed by the metal-working industries—iron, steel, and nonferrous metals—where they are responsible for specifying, controlling, and testing the quality of the metals during manufacture. Others work in industries that manufacture machinery, electrical equipment, aircraft and aircraft parts, and in mining. Some work in federal agencies such as the Bureau of Mines.

The development of new, lightweight metals for use in communications equipment, computers, and spacecraft is a growing field for metallurgical engineers as are the processing and recycling of industrial waste and processing of low-grade ores. Problems associated with the use of nuclear energy will also require the expertise of metallurgists and metallurgical engineers.

Places of Employment and Working Conditions   The work settings of metallurgical engineers vary from the laboratory to smelting and mining locations to factory production lines. Some of these operations are located in remote areas.

Qualifications, Education, and Training   The ability to think analytically, a capacity for detail, and the ability to work as part of a team are all necessary. Good communication skills are important.

Mathematics and the sciences must be emphasized in high school.

A bachelor's degree in engineering is the minimum requirement in this field. In a typical curriculum, the first two years are spent in the study of basic sciences such as physics and chemistry and mathematics, introductory engineering, and some liberal arts courses. The remaining years are usually devoted to specialized engineering courses. Engineering programs can last from four to six years. Those requiring five or six years to complete may award a master's degree or may provide a cooperative plan of study plus practical work experience in a nearby industry.

Because of rapid changes in technology, many engineers continue their education throughout their careers. A graduate degree is necessary for most teaching and research positions and for many management jobs. Some specialties such as nuclear engineering are taught only at the graduate level. Some persons obtain graduate degrees in business administration.

Engineering graduates usually work under the supervision of an experienced engineer or in a company training program until they become acquainted with the requirements of a particular company or industry.

All states require licensing of engineers whose work may affect life, health, or property or who offer their services to the public. Those who are licensed, about one-third of all engineers, are called registered engineers. Requirements include graduation from an accredited engineering school, four years of experience, and a written examination.

Potential and Advancement
There are about 17,000 metallurgical engineers. Substantial growth is expected in this field, providing excellent employment prospects into the 1990s.

Income
Starting salaries for engineers with the bachelor's degree are significantly higher than starting salaries of college graduates in other fields. According to the College Placement Council, engineering graduates with a bachelor's degree and no experience averaged about $27,900 a year in private industry in 1986; those with a master's degree and no experience, $33,100 a year; and those with a Ph.D., $42,200. Starting offers for those with the bachelor's degree vary by branch. Engineers in private industry in 1986 averaged $27,866 at the most junior level, and $79,021 at senior managerials levels. Experienced mid-level engineers with no supervisory responsibilities averaged $42,677.

Additional Sources of Information

The Metallurgical Society of the American Institute of Mining, Metallurgical, and Petroleum Engineers
410 Commonwealth Drive
Warrendale, PA 15086

American Society for Metals
Metals Park, OH 44073

Engineers' Council for Professional Development
345 East 47th Street
New York, NY 10017

National Society of Professional Engineers
1420 King Street
Alexandria, VA 22314

American Society for Engineering Education
11 Dupont Circle
Suite 200
Washington, DC 20036

Society of Women Engineers
United Engineering Center
345 East 47th Street
New York, NY 10017

Meteorologist

The Job   The study of the atmosphere—its physical characteristics, motions, and processes—is the work of meteorologists. Although the best-known application of this study is in weather forecasting, meteorologists are also engaged in research and problem solving in the fields of air pollution, transportation, agriculture, and industrial operations.

Physical meteorologists study the chemical and electrical properties of the atmosphere as they affect the formation of clouds, rain, and snow. *Climatologists* analyze past data on wind, rainfall, and temperature to determine weather patterns for a given area; this work is important in designing buildings and in planning effective land use. *Operational or synoptic meteorologists* study current weather information, such as temperature, humidity, air pressure, and wind velocity, in order to make short- and long-range forecasts.

The largest single employer of civilian meteorologists is the National Oceanic and Atmospheric Administration (NOAA) which employs over 1,800 meteorologists at stations in all parts of the United States and at some locations overseas.

About 3,000 meteorologists work for private industry, including airlines, private weather consulting firms, manufacturers of meteorological instruments, radio and television stations, and the aerospace industry.

Colleges and universities employ about 1,300 meteorologists in teaching and research.

Only about 2 percent of all meteorologists are women, most of them employed by weather bureaus.

Related jobs are: geologist, geophysicist, oceanographer.

Places of Employment and Working Conditions

Meteorologists work in all areas of the United States, but the largest concentrations are in California, Maryland, and the Washington, D.C., area.

Since they continue around the clock, seven days a week, jobs in weather stations entail night and weekend shifts. Some stations are at remote locations and may require the meteorologist to work alone.

Qualifications, Education, and Training

Curiosity, analytical thinking, and attention to detail are necessary qualities for a meteorologist.

High school should include as many science and mathematics courses as are possible.

A bachelor's degree with a major in meteorology or a related field is acceptable for some jobs. Teaching positions, research, and many jobs in private industry require advanced degrees.

The armed forces provide training for meteorologists including advanced training for officers. NOAA also provides advanced training and sponsors cooperative education programs for college students that provide very valuable experience.

Potential and Advancement

There are about 5,600 civilian meteorologists and several thousand members of the armed forces who do forecasting and meteorological work. This is a relatively small job field, and not many degrees are awarded in meteorology. Job opportunities will be fair with the number of job openings just about equal to the number of qualified jobseekers.

Meteorologists with advanced degrees and experience can advance to supervisory and administrative positions.

Income

The average salary for meteorologists employed by the federal government was $39,700 in 1986. In early 1987, meteorologists in the federal government with a bachelor's degree and no experience received starting salaries of $14,822 or $18,358 a year, depending on their college grades. Those with a master's degree could start at $18,358 or $22,458; those with the Ph.D. degree, at $27,172 or $32,567.

Additional Sources of Information

American Geophysical Union
2000 Florida Avenue, NW
Washington, DC 20009

Personnel Operations Branch, AD 41
National Oceanic and Atmospheric Administration
6001 Executive Boulevard
Rockville, MD 20852

American Meteorological Society
45 Beacon Street
Boston, MA 02108

Mining Engineer

The Job   Mining engineers frequently specialize in a specific mineral such as coal or copper. They find, extract, and prepare minerals for manufacturing use.

Some mining engineers work with geologists and metallurgical engineers (see appropriate job descriptions) to locate and appraise new ore deposits. Others design and supervise construction of open-pit and underground mines including mine shafts and tunnels or design methods for transporting minerals to processing plants.

Mining engineers engaged in the day-to-day operations of a mine are responsible for mine safety, ventilation, water supply, power and communication, and equipment maintenance. Direction of mineral processing operations, which requires separating the usable ore from dirt, rocks, and other materials, is also usually the responsibility of a mining engineer.

Some mining engineers specialize in the design and development of new mining equipment. An increasing number work on the reclamation of mined land and on the air and water pollution problems related to mining.

Most mining engineers work in the mining industry. Others work for mining equipment manufacturers or as independent consultants. Federal and state agencies employ mining engineers on regulatory bodies and as inspectors.

Places of Employment and Working Conditions   Most mining engineers work at the location of the mine, usually near small communities in rural areas. Many find employment opportunities overseas.

The work can be hazardous since at least some time is often spent working underground.

Qualifications, Education, and Training

The ability to think analytically, a capacity for detail, and the ability to work as part of a team are all necessary. Good communication skills are important.

Mathematics and the sciences must be emphasized in high school.

A bachelor's degree in engineering is the minimum requirement in this field. In a typical curriculum, the first two years are spent in the study of basic sciences such as physics and chemistry and mathematics, introductory engineering, and some liberal arts courses. The remaining years are usually devoted to specialized engineering courses. Engineering programs can last from four to six years. Those that require five or six years to complete may award a master's degree or may provide a cooperative plan of study plus practical work experience with a nearby industry.

Because of rapid changes in technology, many engineers continue their education throughout their careers. A graduate degree is necessary for most teaching and research positions and for many management jobs. Some persons obtain graduate degrees in business administration.

Engineering graduates usually work under the supervision of an experienced engineer or in a company training program until they become acquainted with the requirements of a particular company or industry.

All states require licensing of engineers whose work may affect life, health, or property or who offer their services to the public. Those who are licensed, about one-third of all engineers, are called registered engineers. Requirements include graduation from an accredited engineering school, four years of experience, and a written examination.

Potential and Advancement

There are about 5,200 mining engineers. Substantial employment growth is expected in this field because of the energy situation, the increased demand for mine safety and advanced mining technology, and the development of oil shale deposits and recovery of metals from the sea.

Income

Starting salaries for engineers with the bachelor's degree are significantly higher than starting salaries of college graduates in other fields. According to the College Placement Council, engineering graduates with a bachelor's degree and no experience averaged about $27,900 a year in private industry in 1986; those with a master's degree and no experience, $33,100 a year; and those with a Ph.D., $42,200. Starting offers for those with the bachelor's degree vary by branch. Engineers in private industry in 1986 averaged $27,866 at the most junior level, and $79,021 at senior managerial levels. Experienced mid-level engineers with no supervisory responsibilities averaged $42,677.

Additional Sources of Information

The Society of Mining Engineers
P.O. Box 625005
Littleton, CO 80127

Engineers' Council for Professional Development
345 East 47th Street
New York, NY 10017

National Society of Professional Engineers
1420 King Street
Alexandria, VA 22314

American Society for Engineering Education
11 Dupont Circle
Suite 200
Washington, DC 20036

Oceanographer

The Job   Using the principles and techniques of natural science, mathematics, and engineering, oceanographers study the movements, physical properties, and plant and animal life of the oceans. They make observations, conduct experiments, and collect specimens at sea that are later analyzed in laboratories. Their work contributes to improving weather forecasting, locating fishing, locating petroleum and mineral resources, and improving national defense.

Most oceanographers specialize in one branch of the science. *Marine biologists* study plant and animal life in the ocean to determine the effects of pollution on marine life. Their work is also important in improving and controlling sport and commercial fishing. *Marine geologists* study underwater mountain ranges, rocks, and sediments of the oceans to locate regions where minerals, oil, and gas may be found. Other oceanographic specialists study the relationship between the sea and the atmosphere and the chemical composition of ocean water and sediments. Others with engineering or electronics training design and build instruments for oceanographic research, lay cables, and supervise underwater construction.

About one-half of all oceanographers work for colleges and universities. In addition to holding teaching positions, they take part in research projects sponsored by universities at sea and in facilities along our coasts.

The United States Navy and the National Oceanic and Atmospheric Administration employ almost one-fourth of all oceanographers. State fisheries employ a few. An increasing number of oceanographers are being employed by private industry, particularly in aquaculture, chemical field, construction, and in oceanographic equipment manufacture.

There are very few women employed as oceanographers.

Related jobs include: chemist, geologist, geophysicist, life scientist, and meteorologist.

Places of Employment and Working Conditions

Most oceanographers work in the states that border the ocean; almost half of all oceanographers work in California, Maryland, and Virginia.

Oceanographers engaged in research that requires sea voyages are often away from home for long periods of time, and they may have to live and work in cramped quarters.

Qualifications, Education, and Training

Anyone interested in this career field should have curiosity and the patience necessary to collect data and do research.

High school should include as many science and mathematics courses as possible. Hobbies or summer jobs that involve boating or ocean fishing are helpful.

A bachelor's degree with a major in oceanography, chemistry, biology, earth or physical sciences, mathematics, or engineering is the first step for a would-be oceanographer and is generally sufficient for entry-level jobs such as research assistant.

Graduate training in oceanography or a basic science is required for most jobs in research and teaching and for all top-level positions; a Ph.D. is required for many. Graduate students usually spend part of their time at sea conducting experiments and learning the techniques of gathering oceanographic information.

Potential and Advancement

There are about 2,800 people employed as oceanographers. This is a relatively small field, and there will be competition for any available job openings. Those who combine training in other scientific or engineering fields with oceanography will have the best chances for employment.

Oceanographers with advanced degrees and experience can advance to administrative or supervisory positions in research laboratories. They may also advance by becoming directors of surveys or research programs.

Income   Surveys by the College Placement Council indicate that graduates with bachelor's degrees in physical and earth sciences received an average starting offer of $19,200 a year in 1986.

In the federal government in early 1987, geologists and geophysicists having a bachelor's degree could begin at $14,822 or $18,358 a year, depending on their college records. Those having a master's degree could start at $18,358 or $22,458 a year; those having the Ph.D. degree, at $27,172 or $32,567. In 1986, the average salary for geologists in the federal government was about $37,500 a year and for geophysicists, about $40,900 a year.

Additional Sources of Information

American Society of Limnology and Oceanography
Virginia Institute of Marine Science
College of William and Mary
Glouster Point, VA 23062

U.S. Civil Service Commission
Washington Area Office
1900 E Street, NW
Washington, DC 20415

International Oceanographic Foundation
3979 Rickenbacker Causeway
Virginia Key
Miami, FL 33149

Operating Engineer

The Job   Operating engineers, who are also called construction machinery operators, operate all kinds of construction equipment. They are usually classified by the type or capacity of the machines they operate.

Heavy equipment operators are highly skilled in the operation of complex machinery such as cranes. They must accurately judge distances and heights while operating the buttons, levers, and pedals that rotate the crane, raise and lower the boom and loadline, and open and close attachments such as steel-toothed buckets or clamps for lifting materials. At times, operators work without being able to see the pickup or delivery point, depending on hand or flag signals from another worker. When constructing new buildings, they work far above the ground.

The operation of medium-sized construction equipment requires fewer controls and is done at ground level. *Bulldozer operators,* for example, lift and lower the blade and move the bulldozer back and forth over the construction area. Trench excavators, paving machines, and other construction equipment are also in this category.

Lightweight equipment such as an air compressor is the simplest to operate. (An air compressor is a diesel engine that takes in air and forces it through a narrow hose. The resulting pressure is used to run special tools.) The operator makes sure the compressor has fuel and water, adjusts and maintains pressure levels, and makes minor repairs.

Operating engineers often work with helpers called *oilers* who keep the equipment properly lubricated and supplied with fuel.

About half of all operating engineers operate excavating, grading, and road machinery; about one-fifth are bulldozer operators; about one-fourth operate cranes, derricks, hoists, air compressors, trench-pipe layers, and dredges.

Most operating engineers work for contractors in large-scale construction projects such as highways, dams, and airports. Others work for utility companies and business firms that do their own construction; state and local highway and public works departments; and in factories and mines using power-driven machinery, hoists, and cranes. Very few operating engineers are self-employed.

The International Union of Operating Engineers is the bargaining unit for many workers in this field.

Places of Employment and Working Conditions

Most operating engineers work outdoors. They work steadily during the warm months but have slow periods in cold months or in bad weather. Operation of medium-sized equipment is physically tiring because of constant movement and the jolting and noise levels of the equipment. Those working on highway construction sometimes work in remote locations.

Qualifications, Education, and Training

Operating engineers need physical stamina, mechanical ability, excellent eyesight and eye-hand coordination, and manual dexterity.

Driver education and automobile mechanics courses in high school are helpful, and experience in operating a tractor or other farm equipment can provide a good background for this work.

A number of private schools offer instruction in the operation of some types of construction equipment, but anyone considering such a school should check with local construction employers for their opinion of the training received by the school's graduates. Not all schools produce suitably trained people.

Most employers prefer to hire operating engineers who have completed a formal apprenticeship program, since they are more thoroughly trained and can operate a variety of equipment. Programs are usually sponsored and supervised by a joint union-management committee; the armed forces also provide apprenticeship programs. An apprenticeship consists of at least three years of on-the-job training plus 144 hours per year of related classroom instruction in hydraulics, engine operation and repair; cable splicing, welding, safety, and first aid.

Apprenticeship applicants usually need a high school or vocational school diploma, but not always. They must be at least 18 years old.

Apprentices start by working as oilers or helpers. They clean, grease, repair and start engines. Within the first year of apprenticeship, they usually begin to perform simple machine operations and progress to more complex operations, always under the supervision of an experienced operating engineer.

Potential and Advancement
There are about 600,000 operating engineers; jobs should be plentiful over the long run for well-trained applicants. Ups and downs in the economy, however, can cause temporary slumps in this industry. Job openings are most plentiful in the spring and early summer in many areas.

Promotion opportunities in this industry are few, but a few operating engineers do advance to supervisory positions.

Income
Wage rates vary depending on the machine operated. Average union rates in metropolitan areas are $10.50 an hour for crane operators (heavy equipment); $10.15 for bulldozer operators (medium-sized equipment); and $9.25 for compressor operators (light equipment). Because of seasonal and bad-weather down periods, annual earnings do not reflect these high hourly rates.

In 1985, the median income for operating engineers was $21,320.

Apprentices start at 70 percent of the hourly rate for experienced workers and receive periodic increases during their training.

Additional Sources of Information

Associated General Contractors of America, Inc.
1957 E Street NW
Washington, DC 20006

International Union of Operating Engineers
1125 17th Street, NW
Washington, DC 20036

Petroleum Engineer

The Job   Petroleum engineers are responsible for exploring and drilling for oil and gas and for efficient production. Some concentrate on research and development into methods to increase the proportion of oil recovered from each oil reservoir.

Most petroleum engineers are employed by the major oil companies and by the hundreds of small, independent oil exploration and production companies. Drilling equipment manufacturers and suppliers also employ petroleum engineers. Engineering consulting firms and independent consulting engineers use their services, and federal and state agencies employ petroleum engineers on regulatory boards and as inspectors.

Banks and other financial institutions sometimes employ petroleum engineers to provide information on the economic value of oil and gas properties.

Places of Employment and Working Conditions   About three-fourths of all petroleum engineers work in California, Louisiana, Oklahoma, and Texas. Many work overseas for U.S. companies and for foreign governments.

This can be dirty work and it is sometimes dangerous. Assignments to offshore oil rigs or remote foreign locations can make family life difficult.

Qualifications, Education, and Training
The ability to think analytically, a capacity for detail, and the ability to work as part of a team are all necessary. Good communication skills are important.

Mathematics and the sciences must be emphasized in high school.

A bachelor's degree in engineering is the minimum requirement in this field. In a typical curriculum, the first two years are spent in the study of basic sciences such as physics and chemistry and mathematics, introductory engineering, and some liberal arts courses. The remaining years are usually devoted to specialized engineering courses. Engineering programs can last from four to six years. Those requiring five or six years to complete may award a master's degree or may provide a cooperative plan of study plus practical work experience with a nearby industry.

Because of rapid changes in technology, many engineers continue their education throughout their careers. A graduate degree is necessary for most teaching and research positions and for many management jobs.

Engineering graduates usually work under the supervision of an experienced engineer or in a company training program until they become acquainted with the requirements of a particular company or industry.

All states require licensing of engineers whose work may affect life, health, or property or who offer their services to the public. Those who are licensed, about one-third of all engineers, are called registered engineers. Requirements include graduation from an accredited engineering school, four years of experience, and a written examination.

Potential and Advancement
There are about 22,000 petroleum engineers, and substantial employment growth is expected in this field. Demand for increased domestic oil and gas resources means increased exploration and production, which will provide many job openings for petroleum engineers.

Income
Starting salaries in private industry average $27,900 with a bachelor's degree; $33,100 with a master's degree; and $42,200 or more with a Ph.D.

The federal government pays beginners $18,710 to $28,039, depending on degree and experience. Average salary for experienced engineers federally employed is about $38,000.

Experienced engineers average $42,677 in private industry; $24,000 to $51,000 for nine-month faculty positions in colleges and universities.

Additional Sources of Information

American Society for Engineering Education
11 Dupont Circle
Suite 200
Washington, DC 20036

Engineers' Council for Professional Development
345 East 47th Street
New York, NY 10017

National Society of Professional Engineers
1420 King Street
Alexandria, VA 22314

Society of Petroleum Engineers of AIME
P.O. Box 833836
Richardson, TX 75083

Society of Women Engineers
United Engineering Center
345 East 47th Street
New York, NY 10017

Photographic Laboratory Technician

The Job   The development of film, preparation of prints and slides, enlarging and retouching of photographs, and other film processing chores are performed by photographic laboratory technicians. They service both the amateur photographer (in labs that mass-process film) and the professional photographer in independent labs or for individual studios.

All-around *darkroom technicians* can perform all tasks necessary to develop and print film including enlarging and retouching. They can handle black-and-white negative, color negative, or color positive work. Since color work is more difficult than black-and-white, some highly skilled technicians specialize as *color technicians*.

Technicians who work in photography studios often function as assistants to the photographer setting up lights and cameras. Many future photographers begin this way, dividing their time between processing film and learning about photography.

In some labs, technicians may be assisted by helpers or assistants who specialize in just one process such as developing or retouching. In large photo labs with automatic film-processing equipment, darkroom technicians supervise semiskilled workers who handle many individual tasks such as film numbering, chemical mixing, or slide mounting.

Places of Employment and Working Conditions   Photographic laboratory technicians are employed in all parts of the country with most job opportunities in large cities.

Photographic laboratory technicians usually work a 40-hour week. In labs that process film for amateur photographers, the summer months and several weeks after the Christmas season require considerable amounts of overtime. Jobs in this field are not physically strenuous, but many of the semiskilled jobs are repetitious and fast-paced; some of the processes can cause eye fatigue.

Qualifications, Education, and Training   Good eyesight and color vision are necessary, as well as manual dexterity.

A high school diploma is not always necessary but can provide a good background. Chemistry and mathematics courses are valuable, and any courses, part-time jobs, or amateur photography and film processing work are helpful.

Most darkroom technicians acquire their skills through on-the-job training, which takes about three years. Others attend trade or technical schools or receive their training in the armed forces.

A few junior and community colleges offer a two-year course in photographic technology leading to an associate degree. College-level training is helpful in securing supervisory and management positions.

Potential and Advancement   There are about 56,000 people employed in some phase of photographic laboratory work. This job field is expected to grow steadily in spite of the increasing use of automated processing equip-

ment and self-processing cameras. Job opportunities for well-trained, all-around darkroom technicians will be best in business and industry and in independent labs that service photographers in specialty fields.

Income Earnings of photo process workers vary greatly depending on skill level, experience, and geographic location. Median earnings for full-time photo process workers in 1986 were about $250 a week. The middle 50 percent earned between $190 and $340 a week. The lowest 10 percent earned less than $160 a week, the highest 10 percent more than $480.

Additional Sources of Information

Photo Marketing Association International
3000 Picture Place
Jackson, MI 49201

Professional Photographers of America, Inc.
1090 Executive Way
Des Plaines, IL 60018

Photographic Art and Science Foundation
111 Stratford Road
Des Plaines, IL 60016

Physicist

The Job Physicists develop theories that describe the fundamental forces and laws of nature. Most physicists work in research and development. Their work in recent years has contributed to progress in such fields as nuclear energy, electronics, communications, aerospace, and medical instrumentation.

Physicists usually specialize in one branch of the science—elementary particle physics; nuclear physics; atomic, electron, and molecular physics; physics of condensed matter; optics; acoustics; plasma physics; or the physics of fluids.

About one-half of all physicists teach or do research in colleges and universities. Private industry employs about one-third of all physicists mainly in companies manufacturing chemicals, electrical equipment, aircraft, and missiles.

About 8,000 physicists work for the federal government, most of them in the Departments of Defense and Commerce.

Only 4 percent of all physicists are women, but this may increase as more high school guidance counselors encourage girls who are good in science and mathematics to enter this field.

Places of Employment and Working Conditions

Physicists are employed in all parts of the country with the heaviest concentrations in industrial areas and areas with large college enrollments. Over one-fourth of all physicists work in the areas in and around New York City, Boston, Washington, D.C., and Los Angeles-Long Beach, California.

Qualifications, Education, and Training

An inquisitive mind, imagination, the ability to think in abstract terms, and mathematical ability are necessary for a physicist.

High school courses in science and mathematics are necessary.

A career in physics usually requires a Ph.D. A bachelor's degree in physics or mathematics is usually the first step followed by a master's degree. Some graduate students are able to work as research assistants while they study for a master's degree and may be hired as instructors while completing the Ph.D. requirements.

Potential and Advancement

There are about 22,000 physicists. The number of graduate degrees awarded in physics has been declining since 1970, and this trend is expected to continue through the 1990s. Most job openings will occur to replace those who retire or leave the field. There will be some growth of job opportunities in the private sector, but job openings in colleges and universities will decline. Those with only a bachelor's degree in physics may become secondary school teachers if they fulfill state teacher certification requirements.

Physicists advance to more complex tasks as they gain experience and may move up to positions as project leaders or research directors; some advance to top management jobs. Physicists who develop new products often form their own companies.

Income

Starting salaries for physicists in private industry averaged about $31,200 a year in 1986 for those with a master's degree and $42,500 for those with a Ph.D., according to an American Institute of Physics survey.

Depending on their college records, physicists with a bachelor's degree started in the federal government in early 1987 at either $14,822 or $18,358 a year. Beginning physicists having a master's degree started at $18,358 or $22,458, and those having the Ph.D. degree began at $27,172 or $32,567. Average earnings for all physicists in the federal government in 1986 were $45,600 a year.

Starting salaries for college and university physics faculty with the Ph.D. averaged $29,500 in 1986, according to the American Institute of Physics. Many faculty physicists supplement their regular incomes with consulting and research projects.

Additional Sources of Information

American Institute of Physics
335 East 45th Street
New York, NY 10017

Interagency Board of U.S. Civil Service Examiners for Washington, D.C.
1900 E Street, NW
Washington, DC 20415

Radiologic (X-Ray) Technologist

The Job   In the medical field, X-ray pictures (radiographs) are taken by radiologic technologists who operate X-ray equipment. They usually work under the supervision of a radiologist—a physician who specializes in the use and interpretation of X-rays.

There are three specialties within the field of radiologic technology; a radiologic technologist works in all three areas.

The most familiar specialty is the use of X-ray pictures to study and diagnose injury or disease to the human body. In this specialty, the technologist positions the patient and exposes and develops the film. During fluoroscopic examinations (watching the internal movements of the body organs on a screen or monitor), the technologist prepares solutions and assists the physician.

The second specialty area is nuclear medicine technology—the application of radioactive material to aid in the diagnosis and treatment of illness or injury.

Working under the direct supervision of a radiologist, the technologist prepares solutions containing radioactive materials that will be absorbed by the patient's internal organs and show up on special cameras or scanners. These materials trace the course of a disease by showing the difference between healthy and diseased tissue.

Radiation therapy—the use of radiation-producing machines to provide therapeutic treatments—is the third specialty. Here, the technology works under the direct supervision of a radiologist, applying the prescribed amount of radiation for a specified length of time.

During all these procedures, the technologist is responsible for the safety and comfort of the patient and must keep accurate and complete records of all treatments. Technologists also schedule appointments and file X-rays and the radiologist's evaluations.

About three-quarters of all radiological technologists work in hospitals. The remainder work in medical laboratories, physicians' and dentists' offices, federal and state health agencies, and public school systems.

Many women work in this field. School systems and physicians' offices provide some opportunities for part-time work, which makes the field attractive to people with family responsibilities.

Places of Employment and Working Conditions   Radiologic technologists are found in all parts of the country in towns and cities of all sizes. The largest concentrations are in cities with large medical centers and hospitals.

Full-time technologists usually work a 40-hour week. Those employed in hospitals that provide 24-hour emergency coverage have some shift work or may be on call. There are potential radiation hazards in this field, but careful attention to safety procedures and the use of protective clothing and shielding devices provide protection.

Qualifications, Education, and Training   Anyone considering this career should be in good health, be emotionally stable, and be able to work with people who are injured or ill. The job also requires patience and attention to detail.

A high school diploma or its equivalent is required for acceptance into an X-ray technology program. Programs approved by the American Medical Association are offered by many hospitals, medical schools affiliated with hospitals, colleges and universities, vocational and technical schools, and by the armed forces. The programs vary in length from two to four years; a bachelor's degree in radiologic technology is awarded after completion of the four-year course.

These training programs include courses in anatomy, physiology, nursing procedures, physics, radiation protection, film processing medical terminology and ethics, radiographic positioning and exposure, and department administration.

Although registration with the American Registry of Radiologic Technologists is not required for work in this field, it is an asset in obtaining highly skilled and specialized positions. Registration requirements include completion of an approved program of medical X-ray technology and a written examination. The technologist may then use the title registered technologist (ARRT). Once registered, technologists may be certified in radiation therapy or nuclear medicine by completing an additional year of education.

Potential and Advancement
There are about 115,000 radiological technologists at the present time. Employment in this field, as in all medical fields, is expected to expand rapidly; the number of graduates, however, is also expected to grow rapidly. If this trend continues, competition will develop for the choicest jobs, as the number of applicants catches up with the number of job openings.

In large X-ray departments, technologists can advance to supervisory positions or qualify as instructors in X-ray techniques. There is more opportunity for promotion for those having a bachelor's degree.

Income
Starting salaries of radiologic technologists employed in hospitals, medical schools, and medical centers averaged about $17,200 a year in 1986, according to a national survey by the University of Texas Medical Branch. Experienced radiologic technologists averaged about $22,800 a year.

Workers with specialized skills earn more. Radiation therapy technologists started at about $19,800, according to the University of Texas survey. Experienced radiation therapy technologists averaged $25,000.

Additional Sources of Information

The American Society of Radiologic Technologists
15000 Central Avenue, SE
Albuquerque, NM 87123

Safety Engineer

The Job   The specific duties of safety engineers (also called occupational safety and health specialists) vary depending on where they work. In general, they are responsible for the safe operation of their employer's facilities and for the physical safety of the employees. They inspect, advise, and train.

In a large manufacturing plant, a safety engineer might develop a comprehensive safety program covering thousands of employees. This would include making a detailed analysis of each job, identifying potential hazards, investigating accidents to determine causes, designing and installing safety equipment, establishing safety training programs, and supervising any employee safety committees.

In a trucking company, a safety engineer inspects heavy rigs such as trucks and trailers; checks out drivers for safe driving practices; and studies schedules, routes, loads, and speeds to determine their influence on accidents. In a mining company, a safety engineer inspects underground or openpit areas for compliance with state and federal laws, designs protective equipment and safety devices and programs, and leads rescue activities in emergency situations.

Safety engineers are also concerned with product safety. They work with design engineers to develop products that meet safety standards and monitor manufacturing processes to ensure the safety of the finished product.

Other occupational safety and health specialists work as *fire protection engineers* who safeguard life and property from fire, explosion, and related hazards. Some specialists research the causes of fires and the flammability of different building materials. Others identify hazards and develop protective measures and training programs. They work for fire equipment manufacturers, insurance rating bureaus, and consulting firms. Some are specialists in sprinkler or fire-detection systems.

Industrial hygienists detect and remedy industrial problems that affect the health of workers. They monitor noise levels, dust, vapors, and radioactivity levels. Some work in laboratories and study the effects of various industrial substances on humans and on air and water. They work with government regulatory agencies, environmental groups, and labor organizations, as well as plant management.

Loss control consultants and *occupational health consultants* work for property-liability insurance companies. The services they provide include inspecting the premises for safety violations and giving advice, designing safety training programs, and designing plant health and medical programs. They also work with the insurance company's underwriters to assess risks and develop premium schedules.

Related jobs are: claim representative, engineering and science technician, environmentalist, firefighter, industrial designer, underwriter.

Places of Employment and Working Conditions   Safety engineers and other occupational and health specialists work throughout the country with the largest concentrations in heavily industrialized areas.

These jobs are usually very active and often entail climbing and other strenuous activities in the course of inspections or emergency situations. A great deal of travel is involved for some workers, especially those who work as consultants for insurance companies.

Qualifications, Education, and Training   Safety engineers and other safety and health specialists must have good communications skills and be able to motivate people. They should get along well with people and be able to deal with them effectively at all levels—from company president to production line worker. They should be assertive and have good judgment. Good physical condition is important.

A college preparatory course should be taken in high school with emphasis on mathematics and science.

Graduates of two-year colleges are sometimes hired to work as technicians in this field, but most employers require at least a bachelor's degree in science or engineering. Some prefer a more specialized degree in a field such as industrial safety, safety management, or fire protection engineering or graduate work in industrial hygiene, safety engineering, or occupational safety and health engineering.

Technological advancements make continuing education a necessity in this field. Many insurance companies offer training seminars and correspondence courses; the Occupational Safety and Health Administration conducts courses in occupational injury investigation and radiological health hazards.

After having successfully completed examinations and the required years of experience, specialists in occupational health and safety may achieve certification from their respective professional societies. These designations include certified safety professional; certified industrial hygienist; and member, Society of Fire Protection Engineers.

Potential and Advancement   About 28,000 people work in this field. Employment of occupational safety and health specialists is expected to grow substantially because of changes in government regulations, the growth of

unions, and rising insurance costs. Most job openings will occur in manufacturing and industrial firms.

In large companies, advancement to top-level management is possible for experienced occupational safety and health specialists.

Income   Beginning salaries range from $21,000 to $35,000 a year. Experienced workers earn about $33,882, corporate level executives earn a median income of $57,000 or more.

Additional Sources of Information

American Society of Safety Engineers
1800 East Oakton
Des Plaines, IL 60018

American Industrial Hygiene Association
475 Wolf Ledges Parkway
Akron, OH 44311

Society of Fire Protection Engineers
60 Batterymarch Street
Boston, MA 02110

Division of Training and Manpower Development
National Institute for Occupational Safety and Health
Robert A. Taft Laboratories
4676 Columbia Parkway
Cincinnati, OH 45226

Soil Conservationist

The Job   Soil conservationists provide technical advice to farmers, ranchers, and others on soil and water conservation as well as land erosion.

Most soil conservationists are employed by the federal government in the Department of Agriculture's Soil Conservation Service or in the Department of Interior's Bureau of Indian Affairs. They act as advisors for Soil and Water

Conservation Districts throughout the United States; or work in or near Indian reservations, which are located mainly in the western states.

Other soil conservationists work for state and local governments, public utilities, lumber and paper companies with large holdings of forested lands, and lending institutions in rural areas.

Related jobs are: soil scientist, range manager, farmer.

Places of Employment and Working Conditions
Soil conservationists work throughout the United States.

Most of their work is done outdoors.

Qualifications, Education, and Training
A soil conservationist should have good communication skills, an analytical mind, and a liking for outdoor work.

High school courses should include chemistry and biology.

Soil conservationists usually have a bachelor's degree with a major in soil conservation, agronomy (interaction of plants and soils), or related fields of natural resource sciences such as wildlife biology or forestry. Courses in agricultural engineering and cartography (map-making) are also helpful.

An advanced degree is usually necessary for college teaching and research positions.

Potential and Advancement
There are about 7,500 soil conservationists. Although there will be steady growth of job opportunities in this field, the relatively small size of the field will mean competition for available openings.

Advancement is limited. Conservationists working at the county level can move up to state positions.

Income
Most graduates entering the federal government as foresters, range managers, or soil conservationists in 1987 with a bachelor's degree started at $14,800 a year. Those with a master's degree could start at $22,500. Holders of doctorates could start at $27,200 or, in research positions, at $32,600. In 1986, the average federal salary for foresters was $32,800; for range conservationists, $28,500; and for soil conservationists, $29,600.

Salaries in state and local government and in private industry were generally lower.

Additional Sources of Information

U.S. Civil Service Commission
Washington, DC 20415

Soil Conservation Service
Department of Agriculture
Washington, DC 20250

American Society of Agronomy
677 South Segoe Road
Madison, WI 53711

Soil Scientist

The Job   Soil scientists study the physical, chemical, biological, and behavioral characteristics of soils. Their work is important to farmers, builders, fertilizer manufacturers, real estate appraisers, and lending institutions.

A large part of soil science has to do with categorizing soils according to a national classification system. Once the soils in an area have been classified, the soil scientist prepares a map that shows soil types throughout the area.

A builder who wants to erect a factory or an apartment building will consult a "soil-type" map to locate a spot with a secure base of firm soils. Farmers also consult soil-type maps. Some communities require a certified soil scientist to examine the soil and test the drainage capabilities of any building lot that will be used with a septic system.

Some soil scientists conduct research into the chemical and biological properties of soil to determine what crops grow best in which soils. They also test fertilizers and soils to determine ways to improve less productive soils. Soil scientists are also involved in pollution control programs and soil erosion prevention programs.

More than half of all soil scientists are employed by the Soil Conservation Service of the U.S. Department of Agriculture. Others are employed by the state agricultural experiment stations and agricultural colleges. Private institutions and industries that employ soil scientists include fertilizer companies, land appraisal firms, farm management agencies, and lending institutions such as banks and insurance companies.

Related jobs are: soil conservationist, farmer, range manager.

Places of Employment and Working Conditions   Soil scientists work in every state and in most counties of the United States.

They spend much of their time doing fieldwork in a particular area—usually a county. During bad weather they work indoors preparing maps and writing reports. Soil scientists involved in research usually work in greenhouses or small farm fields.

Qualifications, Education, and Training   An interest in science and agriculture is necessary as well as a liking for outdoor work. Writing skills are also important.

High school courses should include chemistry and biology.

A bachelor's degree with a major in soil science or a closely related field such as agriculture or agronomy (interaction of plants and soils) is necessary. Courses in chemistry and cartography (mapmaking) are also important.

An advanced degree is necessary for many of the better-paying research positions.

Some states require certification of soil scientists who inspect soil conditions prior to building or highway construction. Certification usually entails a written examination plus specified combinations of education and experience.

Potential and Advancement   There are about 2,500 soil scientists. Job openings in this rather small field usually occur to replace those who leave the field or retire, although some limited growth will probably occur.

Soil scientists who have been trained in both fieldwork and laboratory research will have the best opportunities for advancement, especially if they have an advanced degree.

Income   According to the College Placement Council, beginning salary offers for agricultural scientists with a bachelor's degree averaged $19,200 a year in 1986.

In the federal government in 1987, agricultural scientists with a bachelor's degree could start at $14,822 or $18,358 a year, depending on their college records. Those having a master's degree could start at $18,358 a year or $22,458, depending on their academic records or work experience; and those with a Ph.D. degree could begin at $27,172 or $32,567 a year. Agricultural scientists in the federal government averaged about $35,400 a year in 1986.

Additional Sources of Information

U.S. Civil Service Commission
Washington, DC 20415

Soil Conservation Service
U.S. Department of Agriculture
Washington, DC 20205

American Society of Agronomy
677 South Segoe Road
Madison, WI 53711

Statistician

The Job Statisticians gather and interpret numerical data and apply their knowledge of statistical methods to a particular subject area such as economics, human behavior, natural science, or engineering. They may predict population growth, develop quality-control tests for manufactured products, or help business managers and government officials make decisions and evaluate programs.

Statisticians often obtain information about a group of people or things by surveying a portion of the whole. They decide where to gather the data, determine the size and type of the sample group, and develop the survey questionnaire or reporting form. Statisticians who design experiments prepare mathematical models to test a particular theory. Those in analytical work interpret collected data and prepare tables, charts, and written reports on their findings. Mathematical statisticians use mathematical theory to design and improve statistical methods.

Most statisticians are employed in private industry: in manufacturing, public utilities, finance, and insurance companies. The federal government employs about one-eighth of all statisticians, primarily in the Departments of Commerce, Education, Health and Human Services, Agriculture, and Defense. The remaining statisticians are employed by state and local government and colleges and universities.

About one-third of all statisticians are women.

Places of Employment and Working Conditions Statisticians work in all parts of the country; most are in metropolitan areas, especially

New York City, Washington, D.C., and the Los Angeles-Long Beach, California, areas.

Qualifications, Education, and Training
Statisticians must have good reasoning ability, persistence, and the ability to apply basic principles to new types of problems.

High school courses in mathematics are important.

A bachelor's degree with a major in statistics or mathematics is the minimum requirement for this field. A bachelor's degree with a major in a related field such as economics or natural science with a minor in statistics is preferred for some jobs.

Teaching positions and many jobs require graduate work in mathematics or statistics, and courses in computer use and techniques are becoming increasingly important. Economics and business administration courses are also very helpful.

Potential and Advancement
There are about 18,000 statisticians, and the field is expected to grow substantially. Those who combine training in statistics with knowledge of a field of application will have the best job opportunities to choose from.

Opportunities for promotion in this field are best for those with advanced degrees. Experienced statisticians may advance to positions of greater technical responsibility and to supervisory positions.

Income
In the federal government in 1987, the average starting salary of statisticians who had the bachelor's degree and no experience was $14,800 or $18,400 a year, depending on their college grades. Beginning statisticians with the master's degree averaged $22,500 or $27,200. Those with the Ph.D. began at $27,200 or $32,600. The average annual salary for statisticians in the federal government was about $39,400 in 1986.

According to a 1985 survey by the National Science Foundation, the median annual salary of statisticians with a doctoral degree was about $43,700; in business and industry, $43,900; in educational institutions, $42,200; and in the federal government, $47,100.

Salaries in private industry were generally lower than those in the federal government, according to the limited data available.

Additional Sources of Information

American Statistical Association
1429 Duke Street
Alexandria, VA 22314

Interagency Board of U.S. Civil Service Examiners for Washington, DC
1900 E Street, NW
Washington, DC 20414

Institute of Mathematical Statistics
3401 Investment Boulevard
Suite 7
Hayward, CA 94545

Surveyor

The Job   Surveyors measure construction sites, establish official land boundaries, assist in setting land valuations, and collect information for maps and charts.

Most surveyors serve as leaders of surveying teams; they are in charge of the field party and responsible for the accuracy of its work. They record the information disclosed by the survey, verify the accuracy of the survey data, and prepare the sketches, maps, and reports.

A typical field party consists of the *party chief* and three to six assistants and helpers. *Instrument workers* adjust and operate surveying instruments and compile notes, sketches, and records of the data obtained from the instruments. *Chain workers* use steel tape or surveyor's chain to measure distances between surveying points; they usually work in pairs and may mark measured points with pointed stakes. *Rod workers* use a level rod, range pole, or other equipment to assist instrument workers in determining elevations, distances, and directions. They hold and move the range pole according to hand or voice signals from the instrument worker and remove underbrush from the survey line.

Surveyors often specialize in highway surveys; land surveys to establish boundaries (these also require the preparation of maps and legal descriptions for deeds and leases); or topographic surveys to determine elevations, depressions, and contours and the location of roads, rivers, and buildings. Other specialties are mining, pipeline, gravity, and magnetic surveying.

Photogrammetrists measure and interpret photographs to determine various characteristics of natural or man-made features of an area. They apply analytical processes and mathematical techniques to aerial, space, ground, and underwater photographs to prepare detailed maps of areas that are inaccessible or difficult to survey. Control surveys on the ground are then made to determine the accuracy of the maps derived from photogrammetric techniques.

Federal, state, and local government agencies employ about 25 percent of all surveyors. Those who work for state and local governments usually work for highway departments and urban planning and development agencies. Those who work for the federal government are in the U.S. Geological Survey, Bureau of Land Management, Army Corps of Engineers, and the Forest Service.

Many surveyors work for construction companies, engineering and architectural consulting firms, public utilities, and petroleum and natural gas companies. Others own or work for firms that conduct surveys for a fee.

Places of Employment and Working Conditions   Surveyors work throughout the United States.

Surveying is outdoor work with surveyors often walking long distances or climbing hills carrying equipment and instruments. They usually work an eight-hour, five-day week, but may work much longer hours in summer months when conditions are more favorable for surveying.

Qualifications, Education, and Training   Surveyors should be in good physical condition. They need good eyesight, coordination, and hearing and must have the ability to visualize and understand objects, distances, sizes, and other abstract forms. They also need mathematical ability.

High school courses should include algebra, geometry, trigonometry, drafting, and mechanical drawing.

Surveyors acquire their skills through a combination of on-the-job training and courses in surveying. Technical institutes, vocational schools, and junior colleges offer one-, two-, and three-year programs in surveying. Many four-year colleges offer some surveying courses, and a few offer a bachelor's degree in surveying.

High school graduates without any training usually start as rod workers. If they complete a surveying course and gain experience, they may advance to chain worker, instrument worker, and finally to party chief. Beginners who have some training usually start as instrument workers and work up to party chief as they gain experience.

Photogrammetrists usually need a bachelor's degree in engineering or the physical sciences.

All states require licensing or registration of land surveyors who are responsible for locating and describing land boundaries. Registration requirements are very strict because, once registered, surveyors can be held legally responsible for their work. Requirements usually include an examination and from three to eight years of surveying experience.

Potential and Advancement   There are about 94,000 surveyors, 23,000 of them registered. In addition, 13,500 engineers are also registered to do land surveying. Job opportunities are expected to grow steadily in this field; extended periods of slow construction activity, however, could cause temporary slow periods.

Advancement in this field depends mainly on accumulation of experience.

Income   In 1986, the median annual earnings for survey technicians who worked full time year round were about $19,800. The middle 50 percent earned between $15,600 and $26,400 a year; 10 percent earned less than $11,400 a year; and 10 percent earned more than $36,200.

In 1987, high school graduates with little or no training or experience earned about $10,816 annually at entry level jobs on survey crews with the federal government. Those with one year of related postsecondary training earned $11,802. Those with an associate degree that included courses in surveying generally started as instrument assistants with an annual salary of $13,248. The average annual salary for federal surveying technicians in 1986 was $18,262. In 1987, persons starting as land surveyors or cartographers with the federal government earned $14,822 or $18,358 a year, depending on their qualifications. The average annual salary for federal land surveyors in 1986 was $29,900 and, for cartographers, $30,900.

Additional Sources of Information

American Congress on Surveying and Mapping
210 Little Falls Street
Falls Church, VA 22046

American Society of Photogrammetry and Remote Sensing
210 Little Falls Street
Falls Church, VA 22046

Systems Analyst

The Job Systems analysts decide what new data need to be collected, the equipment needed to process the data, and the procedure to be followed in using the information within any given computer system. They use various techniques such as cost accounting, sampling, and mathematical model building to analyze a problem and devise a new system to solve it.

Once a system has been developed, the systems analyst prepares charts and diagrams that describe the system's operation in terms that the manager or customer who will use the system can understand. The analyst may also prepare a cost-benefit analysis of the newly developed system. If the system is accepted, the systems analyst then translates the logical requirements of the system into the capabilities of the particular computer machinery (hardware) in use and prepares specifications for programmers to follow. The systems analyst will also work with the programmers to "debug" (eliminate errors from) a new system.

Because the work is complex and varied, systems analysts specialize in either business or scientific and engineering applications. Some analysts improve systems already in use or adapt existing systems to handle additional types of data. Those involved in research, called *advanced systems designers*, devise new methods of analysis.

Most systems analysts are employed by banks, insurance companies, large manufacturing firms, and data processing services. Others work for wholesale and retail businesses and government agencies.

In many industries, all systems analysts begin as computer programmers and are promoted to analyst positions only after gaining experience. In large data processing departments, they may start as junior systems analysts. Many persons enter this occupation after experience in accounting, economics, or business management (for business positions) or engineering (for scientific work).

Fifteen percent of all systems analysts are women, usually promoted from computer programmer positions.

Places of Employment and Working Conditions Job opportunities for systems analysts are mainly concentrated in the Midwest and the Northeast, although opportunities exist throughout the entire country.

Systems analysts usually work a normal 40-hour week with occasional evening or weekend work.

Qualifications, Education, and Training Systems analysts must be able to think logically, to concentrate, and to handle abstract ideas.

They must be able to communicate effectively with technical personnel such as programmers as well as with those who have no computer background.

High school should include as many mathematics courses as possible.

Because job requirements vary so greatly, there is no universally accepted way of preparing for a career as a systems analyst. A background in accounting, business administration, or economics is preferred by employers in business. Courses in computer concepts, systems analysis, and data retrieval techniques are good preparation for any systems analyst.

Many employers require a college degree in computer science, information science, or data processing. Scientifically oriented organizations often require graduate work as well in some combination of computer science and a science or engineering specialty.

Because technological advances in the computer field come so rapidly, systems analysts must continue their technical education throughout their careers. This training usually takes the form of one- and two-week courses offered by employers, by computer manufacturers, and by softwear (computer systems) vendors.

The Institute for Certification of Computer Professionals confers the designation of certified in data processing (CDP) on systems analysts who have five years of experience and who successfully complete an examination.

Potential and Advancement
There are about 331,000 systems analysts. This job field is expected to grow steadily because of the expanding use of computers. College graduates who have had courses in computer programming, systems analysis, and data processing will have the best opportunities, while those without a degree may face some competition for the available jobs that don't require a degree.

Systems analysts can advance to jobs as lead systems analysts or managers of systems analysis or data processing departments.

Income
Median annual earnings of systems analysts who worked full time in 1986 were about $32,800. The middle 50 percent earned between $25,600 and $41,300 a year. The lowest 10 percent earned less than $19,200; the highest tenth, more than $51,300.

In the federal government, the entrance salary for recent college graduates with a bachelor's degree was about $14,800 a year in 1987. The average annual salary for systems analysts in the federal government was about $32,700 in 1986.

Systems analysts working in the Northeast had the highest earnings and those in Midwest, the lowest. Salaries tend to be highest in mining and public utilities and lowest in finance, insurance, and real estate.

Additional Sources of Information

American Federation of Information Processing Societies
1899 Preston White Drive
Reston, VA 22091

Association for Systems Management
24587 Bagley Road
Cleveland, OH 44138

The Institute for Certification of Computer Professionals
2200 East Devon Avenue
Suite 268
Des Plaines, IL 60018

Technical Writer

The Job   Writers who specialize in preparing scientific and technical material are much in demand. Technical writers may write for the professional members of a special field, detailing new developments and the work of others in the same field. On other assignments, the writer may write for those outside the field—the general public, equipment users, company officers, and stockholders.

Technical writers also prepare operating manuals, catalogs, and instructional materials for manufacturers of scientific equipment. This material is used by company salespeople, technicians who install and maintain the equipment, and the persons who operate the equipment. Writing manuals and training aids for military equipment and weapons is a highly specialized segment of this field.

Research laboratories employ many technical writers who report on the results of research projects. Others write proposals—requests for money or facilities to do research, conduct a project, or develop a prototype of a new product.

Technical writers also write technical books, articles for popular and trade magazines and newspapers, and prepare advertising copy and press releases.

Technical writers are employed by firms in many industries, with the largest numbers working for electronics, aviation, aerospace, weapons, chemical, pharmaceutical, and computer-manufacturing industries. The energy, communications, and computer-software fields are employing increasing numbers of technical writers.

The federal government employs many technical writers in the Departments of the Interior; Agriculture; Health, Education, and Welfare; and the National Aeronautics and Space Administration. The largest federal employer of technical writers, however, is the Department of Defense.

Publishing houses employ substantial numbers of technical writers and *techical editors.* These companies publish business and trade publications and professional journals in engineering, medicine, physics, chemistry, and other sciences. Textbook publishers also employ technical writers and editors.

Many technical writers work as freelancers, sometimes in addition to holding a full-time technical writing job.

Most people do not enter this field directly from college. They usually spend several years or longer working as technicians, scientists, and engineers, research assistants, or teachers before turning to technical writing or editing.

Places of Employment and Working Conditions   Technical writers are employed throughout the country with the largest concentrations in the Northeast, Texas, and California. Working hours are usually about 40 hours a week, but meeting deadlines can mean added hours.

Qualifications, Education, and Training   In addition to having writing skills and scientific or technical knowledge, a technical writer should be logical, accurate, able to work alone or as part of a team, and have disciplined work habits.

High school courses should develop writing skills and must include science and mathematics.

Technical writers come from a variety of educational backgrounds. Some employers prefer a degree in English, journalism, or technical communications plus course work or experience in a specific scientific or technical subject. Others prefer a degree in an appropriate science or in engineering with a minor in journalism or technical communications.

Only ten colleges and universities offer a bachelor's degree in technical writing; four others offer an associate degree. Six schools offer a master's degree program and one a Ph.D. Many journalism, communications, and language and literature programs, however, include appropriate technical writing courses, some given in close cooperation with scientific and engineering departments of the college.

Many technical workshops and seminars, usually intensive one- and two-week courses, are also available at colleges and universities throughout the country.

Potential and Advancement There are about 25,000 technical writers, and the field is expanding. Job opportunities will be best for talented writers with education in a specific scientific or technical field. Opportunities for federal employment have been declining and will probably continue to do so.

Technical writers can move up to technical editor or to supervisory and management positions. Some advance by opening their own firms where they handle technical writing assignments plus industrial publicity and technical advertising.

Income In 1986, beginning salaries for writers and editorial assistants ranged from $18,400 to $29,300 annually, according to surveys by the Executive Compensation Service. Salaries for experienced writers and researchers generally ranged between $20,500 and $36,500 a year, depending on their qualifications and the size of the publication on which they worked. Technical writers had salaries ranging from $19,300 to $37,800.

Writers and editors employed by the federal government earned an average of $28,000 a year in 1986.

Additional Sources of Information

Society for Technical Communication, Inc.
815 15th Street, NW
Suite 506
Washington, DC 20005

American Medical Writers Association
9650 Rockville Pike
Bethesda, MD 20814

Urban Planner

The Job Urban planners develop plans and programs to provide for the future growth of a community; revitalize run-down areas of a community; and achieve more efficient uses of the community's land, social services, industry, and transportation.

Before preparing plans or programs, urban planners conduct detailed studies of local conditions and current population. After preparing a plan, they develop cost estimates and other relevant materials and aid in the presentation of the program before community officials, planning boards, and citizens' groups.

Most urban planners (also called city planners, community planners, or regional planners) work for city, county, or regional planning agencies. State and federal agencies employ urban planners in the fields of housing, transportation, and environmental protection. Large land developers also employ urban planners, and some teach in colleges and universities.

Many urban planners do consulting work, either part time in addition to a regular job, or full time for firms that provide planning services to private developers and government agencies.

About 10 percent of the urban planners working in the United States are women.

Related jobs are: architect, engineer, and landscape architect.

Places of Employment and Working Conditions   Urban planners are employed throughout the United States in communities of all sizes.

A 40-hour workweek is usual for urban planners, but evening and weekend hours are often necessary for meetings and community activities.

Qualifications, Education, and Training   The ability to analyze relationships and to visualize plans and designs are necessary for urban planners. They should be able to work well with people and cooperate with those who may have different viewpoints.

High school students interested in this field should take social science and mathematics courses. Part-time or summer jops in community government offices can be helpful.

Almost all jobs in this field require a master's degree in urban or regional planning, even for entry-level positions. Most graduate programs require two or three years to complete, but students with a bachelor's degree in architecture or engineering can sometimes complete the work in one year. Part-time or summer work in a planning office is usually a required part of the advanced degree program.

Urban planners seeking employment with federal, state, or local governments usually must pass civil service examinations before securing a position.

Potential and Advancement   There are about 20,000 urban planners at work in the United States. This field is expected to grow slowly, but the extent of the growth will depend on the amount of money available for urban planning projects. Federal aid to state and local governments for slum clearance,

smog and traffic control, and urban renewal programs should provide many job opportunities for urban and regional planners. Jobs in the environmental and social services fields will also be available to those with urban planning experience.

Experienced urban planners may be promoted to positions as planning directors where they recommend policy and have greater budget responsibilities. The usual method of advancement, however, is by transfer to a larger community where the problems are more complex and the responsibilities greater.

Income   According to a 1985 survey by the APA, urban and regional planners earned a median annual salary of about $34,100. The median annual salary of planners in city, county, and other local governments was $31,100; in state governments, $33,500; in private consulting firms, $40,100; in business, $40,100; and in nonprofit foundations, $34,100. For planners with over 10 years' experience, county and joint city/county agencies paid about $37,700 annually, while private businesses and consulting firms paid about $48,100.

Additional Sources of Information

American Planning Association
1776 Massachusetts Avenue, NW
Washington, DC 20036

American Society of Planning Officials
1776 Massachusetts Avenue, NW
Washington, DC 20036

Veterinarian

The Job   Doctors of veterinary medicine diagnose, treat, and control diseases and injuries of animals. They treat animals in hopitals and clinics and on farms and ranches. They perform surgery and prescribe and administer drugs and vaccines.

While most familiar to the general public are those veterinarians who treat small animals and pets exclusively (about one-third of all veterinarians), others specialize in the health and breeding of cattle, horses, and other farm animals. Veterinarians are also employed by federal and state public health programs where they function as meat and poultry inspectors. Others teach at veterinary colleges; do research on animal foods, diseases, and drugs; or take part in medical research for the treatment of human diseases. Veterinarians are also employed by zoos, large animal farms, horse-racing stables, and drug manufacturers.

In the army, the air force, and the U.S. Public Health Service, veterinarians are commissioned officers. Other federally employed veterinarians work for the Department of Agriculture.

Only about 3 percent of all veterinarians are women. Since 1970, however, the number of women veterinarians has increased greatly as veterinary colleges have developed more equitable admission policies. Women should find this an excellent career field with many job opportunities, but they must be well prepared educationally to meet the stiff competition for the limited number of places available in veterinary schools.

Places of Employment and Working Conditions   Veterinarians are located throughout the country—in rural areas, small towns, cities, and suburban areas.

Working hours are often long and irregular, and those who work primarily with farm animals must work outdoors in all kinds of weather. In the course of their work, all veterinarians are exposed to injury, disease, and infection.

Qualifications, Education, and Training   A veterinarian needs the ability to get along with animals and should have an interest in science. Physical stamina and a certain amount of strength are also necessary.

High school students interested in this field should emphasize science courses, especially biology. Summer jobs that involve the care of animals can provide valuable experience.

The veterinary degree program (D.V.M. or V.M.D.) requires a minimum of six years of college: at least two years of preveterinary study with emphasis on physical and biological sciences followed by a four-year professional degree program. A few veterinary colleges require three years of preveterinary study, and most applicants complete three to four years of college before entering the professional program.

There are only 27 accredited colleges of veterinary medicine, many of them state supported. Admission to all of these schools is highly competitive with many more qualified applicants than the schools can accept. Successful applicants need preveterinary college grades of ''B'' or better, especially in science courses; part-time work or summer job experience working with animals is a plus. State-supported colleges usually give preference to residents of the state and to applicants from nearby states or regional areas.

The course of study in veterinary colleges is rigorous. It consists of classroom work and practical experience in diagnosing and treating animal diseases, surgery, laboratory work in anatomy and biochemistry, and other scientific and medical studies. Veterinarians who intend to teach or do research usually go on to earn a master's degree in pathology, physiology, or bacteriology.

While a license is not required for federal employment, all other veterinarians must be licensed. Licensing requires a doctor of veterinary degree from an accredited college and written and oral state board of proficiency examinations. Some states will issue licenses without examination to veterinarians licensed by another state.

Potential and Advancement   There are about 37,000 active veterinarians, most of them in private practice. Employment opportunities for veterinarians are excellent primarily because of growth in the population of "companion animals"—horses, dogs, and other pets—and an increase in veterinary research. The growing emphasis on scientific methods of breeding and raising livestock and poultry as well as an increase in public health and disease control programs will also contribute to the demand for veterinarians.

Income   Newly graduated veterinarians working in private practices of established veterinarians typically earned $20,000 to $22,000 in 1986, according to the American Veterinary Medical Association. After 2 to 4 years, earnings rise significantly. The average net earnings of all veterinarians in private practice were about $43,000 in 1985.

Newly graduated veterinarians employed by the federal government started at either $22,500 or $27,200 a year in 1987 depending on their academic record. The average annual salary of veterinarians in the federal government was $41,300 in 1987.

Additional Sources of Information

American Veterinary Medical Association
930 North Meacham Road
Schaumburg, IL 60196

Agricultural Research Service
U.S. Department of Agriculture
Hyattsville, MD 20782

Appendix

Résumés, Application Forms, Cover Letters, and Interviews

You might see a hurdle to leap over, or a hoop to jump through. Or a barrier to knock down. That is how many people think of résumés, application forms, cover letters, and interviews. But you do not have to think of them that way. They are not ways to keep you from a job; they are ways for you to show an employer what you know and what you can do. After all, you are going to get a job. It is just a question of which one.

Employers want to hire people who can do the job. To learn who these people are, they use résumés, application forms, written tests, performance tests, medical examinations, and interviews. You can use each of these different evaluation procedures to your advantage. You might not be able to make a silk purse out of a sow's ear, but at least you can show what a good ear you have.

Creating Effective Résumés and Application Forms

Résumés and application forms are two ways to achieve the same goal: To give the employer written evidence of your qualifications. When creating a résumé or completing an application form, you need two different kinds of information: facts about yourself and facts about the job you want. With this information in hand, you can present the facts about yourself in terms of the job. You have more freedom with a résumé—you can put your best points first and avoid

This article is reprinted from *Occupational Outlook Quarterly*, spring 1987, volume 31, number 1, pp. 17–23, written by Neale Baxter.

blanks. But, even on application forms, you can describe your qualifications in terms of the job's duties.

Know thyself

Begin by assembling information about yourself. Some items appear on virtually every résumé or application form, including the following:

◇ Current address and phone number—if you are rarely at home during business hours, try to give the phone number of a friend or relative who will take messages for you.

◇ Job sought or career goal.

◇ Experience (paid and volunteer)—date of employment, name and full address of the employer, job title, starting and finishing salary, and reason for leaving (moving, returning to school, and seeking a better position are among the readily accepted reasons).

◇ Education—the school's name, the city in which it is located, the years you attended it, the diploma or certificate you earned, and the course of studies you pursued.

◇ Other qualifications—hobbies, organizations you belong to, honors you have received, and leadership positions you have held.

◇ Office machines, tools, equipment you have used, and skills that you possess.

Other information, such as your Social Security number, is often asked for on application forms but is rarely presented on résumés. Application forms might also ask for a record of past addresses and for information that you would rather not reveal, such as a record of convictions. If asked for such information, you must be honest. Honesty does not, however, require that you reveal disabilities that do not affect your overall qualifications for a job.

Know thy job

Next, gather specific information about the jobs you are applying for. You need to know the pay range (so you can make their top your bottom), education and experience usually required, hours and shifts usually worked. Most importantly, you need to know the job duties (so that you can describe your experience in terms of those duties). Study the job description. Some job announcements, especially those issued by a government, even have a checklist that assigns a numerical weight to different qualifications so that you can be certain as to which is the most important; looking at such announcements will give you an idea of what employers look for even if you do not wish to apply for a government job. If the announcement or ad is vague, call the employer to learn what is sought.

Once you have the information you need, you can prepare a résumé. You may need to prepare more than one master résumé if you are going to look for different kinds of jobs. Otherwise, your résumé will not fit the job you seek.

Two kinds of résumés

The way you arrange your résumé depends on how well your experience seems to prepare you for the position you want. Basically, you can either describe your most recent job first and work backwards (reverse chronology) or group similar skills together. No matter which format you use, the following advice applies generally.

◇ Use specifics. A vague description of your duties will make only a vague impression.

◇ Identify accomplishments. If you headed a project, improved productivity, reduced costs, increased membership, or achieved some other goal, say so.

◇ Type your résumé, using a standard typeface. (Printed résumés are becoming more common, but employers do not indicate a preference for them.)

◇ Keep the length down to two pages at the most.

◇ Remember your mother's advice not to say anything if you cannot say something nice. Leave all embarrassing or negative information off the résumé—but be ready to deal with it in a positive fashion at the interview.

◇ Proofread the master copy carefully.

◇ Have someone else proofread the master copy carefully.

◇ Have a third person proofread the master copy carefully.

◇ Use the best quality photocopying machine and good white or off-white paper.

The following information appears on almost every résumé.

◇ Name.

◇ Phone number at which you can be reached or receive messages.

◇ Address.

◇ Job or career sought.

◇ References—often just a statement that references are available suffices. If your references are likely to be known by the person who reads the résumé, however, their names are worth listing.

◇ Experience.

◇ Education.

◇ Special talents.

◇ Personal information—height, weight, marital status, physical condition. Although this information appears on virtually every sample résumé I have ever seen, it is not important according to recruiters. In fact, employers are prohibited by law from asking for some of it. If some of this information is directly job related—the height and weight of a bouncer is important to a disco owner, for example—list it. Otherwise, save space and put in more information about your skills.

Reverse chronology is the easiest method to use. It is also the least effective because it makes when you did something more important than what you can do. It is an especially poor format if you have gaps in your work history, if the job you seek is very different from the job you currently hold, or if you are just entering the job market. About the only time you would want to use such a résumé is when you have progressed up a clearly defined career ladder and want to move up a rung.

Résumés that are not chronological may be called functional, analytical, skill oriented, creative, or some other name. The differences are less important than the similarity, which is that all stress what you can do. The advantage to a potential employer—and, therefore, to your job campaign—should be obvious. The employer can see immediately how you will fit the job. This format also has advantages for many job hunters because it camouflages gaps in paid employment and avoids giving prominence to irrelevant jobs.

You begin writing a functional résumé by determining the skills the employer is looking for. Again, study the job description for this information. Next, review your experience and education to see when you demonstrated the ability sought. Then prepare the résumé itself, putting first the information that relates most obviously to the job. The result will be a résumé with headings such as "Engineering," "Computer Languages," "Communications Skills," or "Design Experience." These headings will have much more impact than the dates that you would use on a chronological résumé.

Fit yourself to a form

Some large employers, such as fast food restaurants and government agencies, make more use of application forms than of résumés. The forms suit the style of large organizations because people find information more quickly if it always appears in the same place. However, creating a résumé before filling out an application form will still benefit you. You can use the résumé when you send a letter inquiring about a position. You can submit a résumé even if an application is required; it will spotlight your qualifications. And the information on the résumé will serve as a handy reference if you must fill out an application form quickly. Application forms are really just résumés in disguise anyway. No matter how rigid the form appears to be, you can still use it to show why you are the person for the job being filled.

At first glance, application forms seem to give a job hunter no leeway. The forms certainly do not have the flexibility that a résumé does, but you can still use them to your best advantage. Remember that the attitude of the person reading the form is not, ''Let's find out why this person is unqualified,'' but, ''Maybe this is the person we want.'' Use all the parts of the form—experience blocks, education blocks, and others—to show that that person is you.

Here's some general advice on completing application forms.

◇ Request two copies of the form. If only one is provided, photocopy it before you make a mark on it. You'll need more than one copy to prepare rough drafts.

◇ Read the whole form before you start completing it.

◇ Prepare a master copy if the same form is used by several divisions within the same company or organization. Do not put the specific job applied for, date, and signature on the master copy. Fill in that information on the photocopies as you submit them.

◇ Type the form if possible. If it has lots of little lines that are hard to type within, type the information on a piece of blank paper that will fit in the space, paste the paper over the form, and photocopy the finished product. Such a procedure results in a much neater, easier to read page.

◇ Leave no blanks; enter n/a (for ''not applicable'') when the information requested does not apply to you; this tells people checking the form that you did not simply skip the question.

◇ Carry a résumé and a copy of other frequently asked information (such as previous addresses) with you when visiting potential employers in case you must fill out an application on the spot. Whenever possible, however, fill the form out at home and mail it in with a résumé and a cover letter that point up your strengths.

Writing Intriguing Cover Letters

You will need a cover letter whenever you send a résumé or application form to a potential employer. The letter should capture the employer's attention, show why you are writing, indicate why your employment will benefit the company, and ask for an interview. The kind of specific information that must be included in a letter means that each must be written individually. Each letter must also be typed perfectly, which may present a problem. Word processing equipment helps. Frequently only the address, first paragraph, and specifics concerning an interview will vary. These items are easily changed on word processing equipment and memory typewriters. If you do not have access to such equipment, you might be able to rent it. Or you might be able to have your letters typed by a résumé or employment services company listed in the yellow pages. Be sure you know the full cost of such a service before agreeing to use one.

Let's go through a letter point by point.

Salutation

Each letter should be addressed by name to the person you want to talk with. That person is the one who can hire you. This is almost certainly not someone in the personnel department, and it is probably not a department head either. It is most likely to be the person who will actually supervise you once you start work. Call the company to make sure you have the right name. And spell it correctly.

Opening

The opening should appeal to the reader. Cover letters are sales letters. Sales are made after you capture a person's attention. You capture the reader's attention most easily by talking about the company rather than yourself. Mention projects under development, recent awards, or favorable comments recently published about the company. You can find such information in the business press, including the business section of local newspapers and the many magazines that are devoted to particular industries. If you are answering an ad, you may mention it. If someone suggested that you write, use their name (with permission, of course).

Body

The body of the letter gives a brief description of your qualifications and refers to the résumé, where your sales campaign can continue.

Closing

You cannot have what you do not ask for. At the end of the letter, request an interview. Suggest a time and state that you will confirm the appointment. Use a standard complimentary close, such as "Sincerely yours," leave three or four lines for your signature, and type your name. I would type my phone number under my name; this recommendation is not usually made, although phone numbers are found on most letterheads. The alternative is to place the phone number in the body of the letter, but it will be more difficult to find there should the reader wish to call you.

Triumphing on Tests and at Interviews

A man with a violin case stood on a subway platform in The Bronx. He asked a conductor, "How do you get to Carnegie Hall?" The conductor replied, "Practice! Practice! Practice!"

Tests

That old joke holds good advice for people preparing for employment tests or interviews. The tests given to job applicants fall into four categories: General aptitude tests, practical tests, tests of physical agility, and medical examinations. You can practice for the first three. If the fourth is required, learn as soon as possible what the disqualifying conditions are, then have your physician examine you for them so that you do not spend years training for a job that you will not be allowed to hold.

To practice for a test, you must learn what the test is. Once again, you must know what job you want to apply for and for whom you want to work in order to find out what tests, if any, are required. Government agencies, which frequently rely on tests, will often provide a sample of the test they use. These samples can be helpful even if an employer uses a different test. Copies of standard government tests are usually available at the library.

If you practice beforehand, you'll be better prepared and less nervous on the day of the test. That will put you ahead of the competition. You will also improve your performance by following this advice:

◇ Make a list of what you will need at the test center, including a pencil; check it before leaving the house.

◇ Get a good night's sleep.

◇ Be at the test center early—at least 15 minutes early.

◇ Read the instructions carefully; make sure they do not differ from the samples you practiced with.

◇ Generally, speed counts; do not linger over difficult questions.

◇ Learn if guessing is penalized. Most tests are scored by counting up the right answers; guessing is all to the good. Some tests are scored by counting the right answers and deducting partial credit for wrong answers; blind guessing will lose you points—but if you can eliminate two wrong choices, a guess might still pay off.

Interviews

For many of us, interviews are the most fearsome part of finding a job. But they are also our best chance to show an employer our qualifications. Interviews are far more flexible than application forms or tests. Use that flexibility to your advantage. As with tests, you can reduce your anxiety and improve your performance by preparing for your interviews ahead of time.

Begin by considering what interviewers want to know. You represent a risk to the employer. A hiring mistake is expensive in terms of lost productivity, wasted training money, and the cost of finding a replacement. To lessen the risk, interviewers try to select people who are highly motivated, understand what the job entails, and show that their background has prepared them for it.

You show that you are highly motivated by learning about the company before the interview, by dressing appropriately, and by being well mannered—which means that you greet the interviewer by name, you do not chew gum or smoke, you listen attentively, and you thank the interviewer at the end of the session. You also show motivation by expressing interest in the job at the end of the interview.

You show that you understand what the job entails and that you can perform it when you explain how your qualifications prepare you for specific duties as described in the company's job listing and when you ask intelligent questions about the nature of the work and the training provided new workers.

One of the best ways to prepare for an interview is to have some practice sessions with a friend or two. Here is a list of some of the most commonly asked questions to get you started.

◇ Why did you apply for this job?

◇ What do you know about this job or company?

◇ Why should I hire you?

◇ What would you do if. . .(usually filled in with a work-related crisis)?

◇ How would you describe yourself?

◇ What would you like to tell me about yourself?

◇ What are your major strengths?

◇ What are your major weaknesses?

◇ What type of work do you like to do best?

◇ What are your interests outside work?

◇ What type of work do you like to do least?

◇ What accomplishment gave you the greatest satisfaction?

◇ What was your worst mistake?

◇ What would you change in your past life?

◇ What courses did you like best or least in school?

◇ What did you like best or least about your last job?

◇ Why did you leave your last job?

◇ Why were you fired?

◇ How does your education or experience relate to this job?

◇ What are your goals?

◇ How do you plan to reach them?

◇ What do you hope to be doing in 5 years? 10?

◇ What salary do you expect?

Many jobhunting books available at libraries discuss ways to answer these questions. Essentially, your strategy should be to concentrate on the job and your ability to do it no matter what the question seems to be asking. If asked for a strength, mention something job related. If asked for a weakness, mention a job-related strength (you work too hard, you worry too much about details, you always have to see the big picture). If asked about a disability or a specific negative factor in your past—a criminal record, a failure in school, being fired—be prepared to stress what you learned from the experience, how you have overcome the shortcoming, and how you are now in a position to do a better job.

So far, only the interviewer's questions have been discussed. But an interview will be a two-way conversation. You really do need to learn more about the position to find out if you want the job. Given how frustrating it is to look for a job, you do not want to take just any position only to learn after 2 weeks that you cannot stand the place and have to look for another job right away. Here are some questions for you to ask the interviewer.

◇ What would a day on this job be like?

◇ Whom would I report to? May I meet this person?

◇ Would I supervise anyone? May I meet them?

◇ How important is this job to the company?

◇ What training programs are offered?

◊ What advancement opportunities are offered?

◊ Why did the last person leave this job?

◊ What is that person doing now?

◊ What is the greatest challenge of this position?

◊ What plans does the company have with regard to. . . ? (Mention some development of which you have read or heard.)

◊ Is the company growing?

After you ask such questions, listen to the interviewer's answers and then, if at all possible, point to something in your education or experience related to it. You might notice that questions about salary and fringe benefits are not included in the above list. Your focus at a first interview should be the company and what you will do for it, not what it will pay you. The salary range will often be given in the ad or position announcement, and information on the usual fringe benefits will be available from the personnel department. Once you have been offered a position, you can negotiate the salary. The jobhunting guides available in bookstores and at the library give many more hints on this subject.

At the end of the interview, you should know what the next step will be: Whether you should contact the interviewer again, whether you should provide more information, whether more interviews must be conducted, and when a final decision will be reached. Try to end on a positive note by reaffirming your interest in the position and pointing out why you will be a good choice to fill it.

Immediately after the interview, make notes of what went well and what you would like to improve. To show your interest in the position, send a followup letter to the interviewer, providing further information on some point raised in the interview and thanking the interviewer once again. Remember, someone is going to hire you; it might be the person you just talked to.